To Patty —

Merry Christmas —

[signature]

"Through the years, Jim Huber has brought compassion and insight to countless assignments. Jim wasn't assigned this story, but more than any other it was one he had to tell."

—Bob Costas, NBC Sports

"Jim Huber has been one of the most eloquent on-air essayists in sports broadcasting history, and now his touching and inspirational book on the death of his father also puts him in a category with the very best writers on the printed page. It's a beautiful story well told by the loving son of a remarkable father facing death with great dignity and courage."

—Leonard Shapiro, Sports Columnist for the *Washington Post*

"Jim Huber is a master at finding the humanity in our heroes. He does it better than ever in this thoughtful tribute to his own hero, his father."

—Jaime Diaz, Senior Writer, *Sports Illustrated*

"I enjoyed a very special relationship with my father. He was not only my father, but also my mentor, my biggest supporter, and my closest friend. To this day, I miss him and that bond we shared. *A Thousand Goodbyes* says many of the things I wish I could have said when my father died. I have known Jim Huber for years, and on both sides of the camera. In this writing, Jim is at his finest. He gives the reader wonderful insight not only into the father but the son as well."

—Jack Nicklaus, Legendary PGA Professional

"Read this warm, wise, and compassionate book and you'll understand why more sports celebrities would rather talk to Jim Huber than almost anyone else in the broadcasting field."

—John Maxim, Author of *The Shadow Box* and *Whistler's Angel*

"Rarely will you ever read a more touching portrait of death making its cruel approach. A son and his father, the son just as I once felt, that my father would always be there. But it is not to be, as Jim Huber so graphically assures us. It is beautiful in its own sad way, yet lovely to see the last bonding of a father and son and their undying love."

—Furman Bisher, Sports Editor of the *Atlanta Journal-Constitution*

a thousand goodbyes

a thousand goodbyes

a son's reflection

on living, dying,

and the things

that matter most

Jim Huber

THOMAS NELSON PUBLISHERS®
Nashville

Published in Nashville, Tennessee, by Thomas Nelson, Inc.

Unless otherwise noted, the Scripture quotations in this publication are from THE NEW KING JAMES VERSION. Copyright © 1979, 1980, 1982, Thomas Nelson, Inc., Publishers.

Library of Congress Cataloging-in-Publication Data

Huber, Jim.
    A thousand goodbyes : a son's reflection on living, dying, and the things that matter most / Jim Huber.
        p. cm.
    ISBN: 0-7852-6688-7
    1. Fathers—Death—Psychological aspects. 2. Fathers and sons. I. Title.

BF789.D4 H69 2001
155.9'37—dc21   2001030634

Printed in the United States of America

01 02 03 04 05 BVG 5 4 3 2 1

To my father. Better late than never.

contents

contents

preface

The day was glorious, bright and shiny and full of promise. If only my golf game could have matched that radiance. I have played the game for years, but on this particular day it was almost as if I had never picked up a club before; if I wasn't pulling the ball left, I was pushing it deep right. My partner and our opponents cringed at my game's disintegration for, though the stakes this day had grown considerably, we were all friends and would likely match up again the next Saturday in a different order.

If I didn't take up crocheting in the meantime.

We were on the sixteenth fairway. Actually, *they* were. I was dead left again and stymied. My ball was sitting between the exposed roots of a giant Georgia pine, which stood directly in my path to the green. I assessed my options, which seemed to be somewhere between slim and none. I could simply pitch it back into the fairway and hope to get up and down for par or I could try to avoid the roots and hook it blindly around the tree, praying that somehow it would find its way home.

Or there was a third possibility.

It would be so easy and no one would ever know. All I had to do was nudge the golf ball a bit to the right, away from the tree, to give myself a perfect line to the green. It's called a "foot wedge" and, who knows, a couple of good ones and I'd nearly be back in the fairway. None of the others in my foursome was near; they were off elsewhere tending to their own problems, probably never giving thought to what might have been going through my mind at that moment. If, however, it had been someone else in there, he would likely have had an escort. One notorious fellow would occasionally join us and, at least once a round, hit one dead into the pines and disappear for a few minutes on his own in search of his ball. Always came the resulting call:

"I found it!" he would yell. "And believe it or not, I have a shot!"

We believed it—and didn't—but grudgingly put up with his waywardness. Cheating is so abhorrent in any form of life, but in golf it is nearly sacrilegious; the game was built hundreds of years ago around the honor system. Yes, you can cheat and you might win, but like anything else, it's the post-cheat that gets you. Try to look your opponent in the eyes or yourself in the mirror. Try to sleep at night. Try to justify it. There's no way.

Still, I was entertaining thoughts of a bit of thievery now. (Frustration will do that to you!) A voice whispered, so slightly that I thought it was the wind in the branches overhead. Perhaps it was.

After looking around and finding no one, I stood back over the ball, pondering my move. I thought of an old comrade, dead and gone now, who had played with holes in the right front pocket of his pants where he always kept a spare golf ball. Whenever he went into the woods after an errant shot and discovered he was in trouble, he would simply work the extra ball down through that hole. It would roll down his pants leg and onto the ground, wherever he wanted it, usually in near-perfect position. One day, someone in another fairway, unbeknownst to this particular fellow, actually stood and watched him do it and the word quickly spread. We continued to play with him but never when it counted for anything. Cheating is a difficult subject to broach with someone you think of as a friend and so, to avoid a conflict, we ignored him . . . but kept a close eye, just the same.

On this day, however, I wondered, what could the harm be in a bit of rearranging? As bad as my fortunes had gone this day, the game owed me something. Almost enough motivation to cut a hole in my pocket . . . but not quite.

The breeze returned in the still of the hot summer afternoon, a murmured admonition: "I'm watching you."

It was my father's raspy voice, as sure as I was facing double bogey. The same playful lilt I had grown to love over the last few decades was masking a very definite threat. I could see him smiling, knowing he had touched me deep inside. He had never in his life played the game of golf, but here he was, in death, enforcing its rules.

"You have a shot?" yelled one of my opponents from across the fairway, snapping me out of my reverie.

"No," I grudgingly answered, looking upward all the while, "no shot. I've gotta pitch out."

"Pity. Too bad." The subsequent snide laughter was part of the ritual.

It has happened so often, in so many differing situations, in the months since my father's death, that it is beyond coincidence. I was raised to recognize an inner conscience but it never had a voice, never had a name, never smiled, until he took over. I had grown to believe that I was my own arbiter, that once I had become old enough to know right from wrong, once the standards had been set,

I would become my own Jiminy Cricket. And whatever I decided was based on my own code of conduct.

Until he died and stepped into the job.

Where is he? Heaven? He surely believed all of his life, and more determinedly in the months of his passing, that would be his final destination. There was no question about it, for it had been something he had begun preparing himself for long, long ago. But if that is the case, heaven is right here in the branches, as I contemplate cheating. Right here in the passenger seat as I consider running the red light. Right here over my shoulder as I work on my expense account. Right here with the soap as my language turns blue. Perhaps he has become my own creation, fulfilling a subconscious need for self-regulation. Maybe I am simply using his memory as a crutch. But if that is the case, then he becomes as real as if he were alive, walking the fairways with me as I play, enjoying nature, wondering why the game has such silly restrictions to begin with.

"Why *can't* you move the ball?" he used to ask seriously. "Who says you can't? It's just a game, isn't it?"

"A game with very strict rules, Dad."

Like life.

I have learned great lessons in the last few years, about dying and living again, lessons only he and I can share. We argue good-naturedly, the dead father and his son, and it must look terribly strange to others watching, me having a very intense discussion with . . . myself, they would surmise. What they cannot know is that arguing with an angel is a grand test of wills, but an awful waste of earth-bound energy.

"I win again." I can hear him laughing now. But, in truth and in tandem, we both win.

He has been physically gone for a while now, the first of my parents to depart. But not a day goes by that I am not reminded, in some way, of the remarkable nature of his passing, of a period of time when he took a tenuous relationship between a father and his elder son and made it whole, healthy, and full of love at long last. In that process, he taught me more about the nature of our existence than in all the decades previous. We explored the rites of dying together, as father and son, as subject and interviewer, and what had always been the most morbid of subjects became acceptable, understood, even fascinating. With a twinkle in his old eyes and a wrinkle of his nose, he took us all along on one of the most incredible journeys toward death . . .

And another life.

chapter one

just never get old

■ SEPTEMBER 1999

The old man's head was propped up on the pillow. His teeth were in a drawer nearby, never to be used again, and so he looked so much like one of those curious folks carved out of old apples; drawn and puckered and humorous. His eyes were closed and his chest wasn't moving and I feared I was too late. It had only been two weeks since I had last seen him and yet the deterioration had me reeling. What was left of his hair had gone from gray to a silvery white, his skin a sickly shade of olive. For the first time, he actually looked like he was dying. Was this really my father? Could he have gone downhill this quickly after all those months of subtle decline?

The red glow from a bedside clock highlighted his left cheek. It was the only color in an otherwise tiny, dark bedroom.

"Dad?"

One eye opened, yellowed from the liver disease, and then the other. Wispy white eyebrows suddenly arched in recognition and he moaned through the tiny cavity that had once held a dentist's creation.

"Oh, you came."

I had to listen carefully, for, without the teeth, each word took on a new formation. It would become a language all its own in the final days, ridiculous and yet worthy of the best linguistic effort.

"You thought I wouldn't?"

He took my hand and held it tight, an unthinkable action just a few years before. His eyes glistened and he smiled wide.

"Oh, I'm so glad. Now I can go in peace."

I had never thought much of my parents dying. I'm not sure why not, for neither seemed exceptionally healthy as they plunged head-long into their seventies, yet their veneer remained bulletproof to me. Perhaps I simply did not want to face it, wanted no part of the whole scene, and so I willed them longevity—demanded it. Even when Dad battled and beat prostate cancer, I never considered death. Even when death became the occasional topic of dinner-table conversation, I still somehow refused to see the inevitability.

"Which one do you suppose will go first?" we would ask, as if we could predict the future.

"Well, you know if Mom goes, Dad will be absolutely lost. It'd probably be best if Dad dies first."

"Probably right, although he'll probably fool us all."

"But then again, if Dad goes first, what a vacuum for Mom. Either way, it's gonna be tough for the one left behind."

Or maybe I'll go first. Yes, that would solve it all. Let *them* do the crying. It wouldn't be the natural order of things, but it would certainly be the perfect cop-out.

Short of doctor-assisted euthanasia or our own hand, we have no say in such matters and so we wait, helplessly, watching for telltale signs, circling lazily like buzzards.

To me, he had always seemed a bit invincible. Even though he had been in and out of hospitals his entire life, poked and cut up for this ailment and that, he never lost that sly smile and the quick wink . . . that "they can't hurt me" look. And I always bought it, wanting badly to.

"You okay, Dad?"

"Me? Oh, yeah, I'm fine."

And then he would screw up his face and frown.

It was his cue. The subsequent exchange became as familiar as passwords opening our hearts to each other:

"Just don't get old," he would say to me.

"I'm not sure I like the alternatives," I would always answer.

And the smile would return, for he didn't particularly care for them, either. But in time that, too, would change. The alternative would grow more attractive and enticing and enduring every moment. He reached that point of not simply resigning but rejoicing. Death would bring new life, renew old acquaintances, end the suffering. You could see the change in his attitude toward that alternative as the months grew into weeks and then days. It seemed almost a mirror of his mother's dwindling days a decade earlier. His father had died first, and as the months turned to years and the walls of the nursing home began to close in, my grandmother's mantra was constant.

"Oh, I just want to go," she would tell us. "I want to join him. I miss him so much. I'm ready to die now."

And so it became, in the final months, with her son, my father. Some would call it "giving in," but I looked deep into his eyes and saw a kind of happiness that could only come with an inner resolution. It would be okay. It was time. If I still had misgivings, uncertainties, about death and all of its seeming finality, he did not. When the word came that his illness was irreversible, that his liver would continue to slowly disintegrate until it resembled a small piece of used charcoal, he accepted his fate and turned his nose toward heaven. He never fought death after that—not once—but began looking forward to it. It was not that simple for his eldest son.

When it became clear that my silent, selfish plea for some kind of eternal life on earth was going unheard (or unanswered) and that he was indeed dying, it came like a blow to the gut, one that lingered and ached for months. My father was *dying* . . . and there was nothing I could do for him. He would soon be gone. Friends, neighbors, coworkers . . . all had lost parents over the years. It seemed such a natural part of life, from the outside looking in. But now I was inside and a combination of fear and desperation began to set in. Surely he would beat this, just as he had all the other problems over the years. Surely God would allow us a little more time together. Just a bit. But there is no negotiating such a bargain in real life and death.

"Are you sure?" I asked the doctor, thinking I would like a second or third or one-hundredth opinion. He could have given me the standard "we all have to go sometime" but, thankfully, he saw the pain in my eyes and treated me kindly. He explained my father's problem, diagrammed the disease, showed me where and when and how and why.

"Well, let's put it this way: he's in bad shape. The liver is disintegrating and because it's so vital to the rest of our system, well . . ."

"Any time frame?"

"Less than a year, more than a month, something in between. That's the best I can do."

"You mean . . ."

"Sorry. It's really not good. Enjoy him as long as you have him."

Dying is an art, rarely done to perfection. Most of us are quite sloppy at it, messy, inarticulate, or bitter. If we have no time for grand exits, if the bus is early or the bullet accurate or the valve slipshod, we leave with much unsaid, a three-act play in the second intermission. Stunned loved ones wander the lobby, left without a finish.

And if we have too much time, we turn sullen and morose. If death could be choreographed by Hollywood, it would be either one final twirl and a collapse, or a lingering crawl, clutching at the dust of the eternal cobblestones. We ought to have the right, as dues-paying citizens of this world, to choose our dramatic departure, though I fear most of us, myself included, would cling frantically to the edge of the cliff through the final three reels. It's easy to say, "Take me quickly," until that time actually comes.

My father managed it just about right . . . just about. There would be some question about that in the last, miserable days, but as he went on his grand and often merry journey, he did it with a style and grace that left us all shaking our heads in astonishment and love. More often than not, we would leave his room after spending time with him, quickly turn a corner and collapse against a wall, tears of grief and laughter mingling in a kind of mourning soup, our breath catching somewhere between a giggle and a gasp.

"Funny thing," he muttered to me, two weeks before the end, and I could hardly wait to find out what could be humorous about such a grisly process. "I thought I'd just be able to close my eyes and, *poof!* I'd be gone. Doesn't work that way."

And then he slowly, agonizingly, worked his weakened arms out from under the covers and raised them high. The skin hung from his bones like graying laundry on a summer line. Looking at me all the while, a devious glint in those eyes, he began to flap his arms.

"Like this. Like an angel."

chapter two

woulda, coulda, shoulda

It was not his fault. He didn't mean to be seventy-eight years old, first and foremost, and he surely didn't figure on the bad batch of blood from the 1950 transfusion destroying his liver nearly fifty years later. But he was and it had, and that was as close as doctors could come to pinpointing the origin of his illness. Age and cirrhosis apparently had been eating away at his insides for years. But when the blood first began to seep from his ears on that dramatic first day of April in 1998, and then from various other parts of his body in the ensuing months, he knew it was only a matter of time. It simply just . . . *appeared*, like an omen. How frightening it must have been to both of my parents; a spot of blood here, one there, no rhyme or reason. Oddly, like a road sign giving directions, the moment of inception remains there today, written in my mother's elegant hand on the calendar she tucked safely away:

"April 1: Bob's ears bleed. See doctor."

At first they thought that his hearing aids had irritated his ears, but it became far more complicated and, in the end, more deadly than that. Throughout April and then May, Dad saw doctor after doctor, six in all, from this clinic to that hospital to this emergency room and so on. They poked and prodded him, took what blood he didn't spill and tested it, yet never were able to put a name to his ailment. At one point, they thought it might have been his spleen and discussed removing it, but finally decided that it wasn't worth the risk. He was too old to handle such an operation. And so they kept at him, eliminating the possibilities as they went. In fact, it wasn't until August, five months later, that they finally decided that, having exhausted everything else, the problem was his liver.

And as was the case with the spleen, he was too old and fragile to even consider a transplant operation. So he would have to just live out his days, slowly deteriorate, and eventually die from cirrhosis of the liver.

Though a common man, Dad had great pride, and when doctors said "liver disease," he made certain they knew he wasn't a drinker. This wasn't going down as suicide, if he had his way. And in the ensuing months, when people asked what he was suffering from, he and my mother invariably answered, "Cirrhosis of the liver—but not the alcoholic kind." Their heads, though bowed, were held high through it all.

He had been a welder in the beginning (because he "liked the colors," as my mother put it), working in the western Pennsylvania steel mills like his grandfather, father, brother, and uncles who were all machinists, a family trade my father only touched on the peripheries. In the end, he was a mailman, like none of them. For twenty-three years, he went bouncing along the back roads of Ocala, Florida, in his little truck, delivering Social Security checks and letters from grandmothers and a daily ration of good cheer. He left them all with a letter in their hands and a smile on their faces. It was as if the very color of those bookend jobs reflected in his countenance. In the days of his millwork, he seemed dark and brooding but in the fresh sunlight, with a stack of catalogs in his hand, he turned bright and radiant. It apparently took him that long to discover he was a "people person," but it was a revelation that changed him for all time.

A good two decades after he had retired from the post office, I was ironically in the home of one of those who had been on his route back then, the adopted mother of a young quarterback destined for the National Football League. She had been working in a clinic when a young, desperate mother had come looking for someone to take care of her brand-new baby. The old widow had already raised a half dozen of her own children, but they were all grown and gone and she was lonely so she agreed to take the child. She raised him as if he were her own, taught him the fear of God, gave him every principle possible, and sent him into the world to become the star he is today.

The tiny shotgun house on the side street was worn and cluttered and falling down around her and the young man had promised to build his surrogate mother a new home with his NFL signing bonus. She was having none of that, determined to live out the rest of her life in this place that had been her home for ages. He was a leading candidate that fall for college's Heisman Trophy and she was going to fly to New York in a few weeks to watch. I had come to listen to her story. We talked as my cameraman set the lights for our interview and I casually mentioned my father having delivered mail along this dirt road years ago.

"What's his name?" she quickly asked, her old eyes lighting up.

"Bob Huber. But you probably don't remember him. That was a long time ago."

"He have black hair, looked kinda dark, like maybe one of us 'cept he wasn't?"

"Oh, yes, in the summertime he got so dark, he coulda passed for just about any race."

"I 'member him. He was a good man, always smilin'. He was the best of 'em all."

I'd like to think she did indeed remember him, like to think he *was* the "best of 'em all." She was a good, God-fearing woman and wouldn't stretch the truth just to make me feel better, would she? After all, do *you* remember the man who brought you your mail twenty-five years ago? Was he light or dark; did he smile large; did he leave an impression along with the letters and bills? But she remembered him, sure enough. Saint Bob, yes, in a blue uniform driving a Postal Service buggy.

He had finally found a calling, a purpose in his life, a reason for being, and it seemed to lift his entire persona. He was a different person, to me at least. But then, I was growing into a man at the same time and so we were in the birthing stage of our adult relationship, at last.

It made little sense, the juxtaposition from the dirty, fire-lit dungeons that were Pittsburgh's steel mills to the fresh air of central Florida, but he had tried a bit of everything in between, sometimes all at once, never able to do much more than work himself to a frazzle. He was an underwater welder in the navy during World War II, working on a repair vessel, but when he returned from the South Pacific, he wanted something more out of life. He was hardly a risk-taker but he knew one thing—he didn't want to stay in the same town as his family all his life, didn't want to work in the same factory, breathe the same stale air, shovel the same sooty snow every interminable winter. He wanted to be somebody, but had no idea how or who.

In his later years, as we grew to become friends for the first time and not distant father and son, he would ride along with me occasionally as I played golf, satisfied simply with sitting in the cart or standing greenside, thinking perhaps of what might have been. A real-life version of Marlon Brando's character in the movie *On the Waterfront*, crying into the wind, "I could've been a contender!" A mental game those of us who never quite get around to contending usually play.

"I caddied some when I was a boy," he would say. "I think I probably coulda been pretty good at this game if I'd had a chance. It was too expensive; I had to work after school; and then when we got married . . ."

We would sit together in the darkness of the den, watching a football game. "I wish I'd played that sport when I was young," he would muse. "I think I coulda been pretty good at it."

Or baseball. Or tennis. Or acting. Or writing. Or anything that he wasn't.

"Woulda, coulda, shoulda." He would chuckle. "Story of my life."

And so, in the beginning, fresh from the war, he drove a cab at night while he went to a Pittsburgh business school but found that he wasn't suited for sales.

"He couldn't sell," my mother says with a laugh today, her eyes misty at the very thought of the man she loved so very long. "He just had a hard time selling things he didn't believe in."

He became a policeman for a while, which seems to me so incongruous now a half century later, for he was hardly the authoritarian type in my mind's eye. I remember, as a tiny child, watching him put his revolver and belt up on a high shelf in the front closet every day upon returning home from directing traffic or whatever it was that he did. Now, looking back at what evolved into a gentle, peaceful, loving man, I wonder if he could have used it. Perhaps that is why his attempt at that particular career was so short-lived, no more than a year. He repaired sewing machines and typewriters, drove delivery trucks with everything from baked goods and bread to milk on board. Though he worked long, often frustrating hours, nothing clicked.

My mother was a strong redhead who once had to settle for second place in the Mrs. Pennsylvania contest because her sorry sewing machine couldn't stitch a straight line—in the days when straight lines and not soft curves made the difference. She kept the family together.

"It was tough," she recalls with a whistle. "Boy, was it! We really struggled for a long time there—all our lives, really. But we got through it with faith and love. That's about all we had. There were times we were down to our last fifty cents and it really took some creative bill-paying.

"He never knew how bad things were. I kept it from him because he'd get, well, kinda paranoid. He'd get upset. So I kept it from him."

Once, when she was the one in the hospital for a change and it was left to my father to take care of the family business, he simply got all the bills together and, one by one, paid as many as their meager bank account would allow. When he ran out of money, he simply let the rest of the bills wait.

"See?" She laughs now. "He didn't have any idea how to juggle. You paid the most important ones and let the others slide a bit. I had become an artist at that. Either file them in the square hole or the circular can. We got into a bit of trouble that month."

And so, back in charge, she managed the family's financial matters.

While he was going from job to job, trying to find a fit, she was not only wife and mother of two young boys but provider as well. Often, she worked two jobs at a time to try to help make ends meet, going from eight in the morning until four in the afternoon, and sliding right into a second job with an hour's break in between; plenty of time to cook dinner and get the laundry done.

So the breadwinning was shared, yet my father seemed the distant observer.

"You wait till your father comes home," was an empty threat most times, for when he finally did, either he was too tired or the indiscretion long forgotten. His thick navy belt hung, menacingly, on the back of their bedroom door as the only physical evidence of what might have been but never was. As a child, I thought of him like that belt, tough and hard-edged, quiet and a bit menacing, though he never once touched me in anger. And he was distant; always around the corner of a door. There are small, sepia-tone photographs in long-forgotten albums of us at the beach, in the mountains, at Christmas, and we are smiling in them, but when I think of him in those days, there is a chill. I don't remember many of his smiles. How odd and sad, for the man I grew to know decades later was a polar opposite, full of warmth and caring, a gentle grin always belying whatever was going on inside him. I long for life's mulligan, to go back and revisit this time and see which of us had changed the most. Perhaps neither. Perhaps both.

They were both strong disciplinarians, though stretched on different frames. Dad was simply a dark figure, a threat never made good. So Mom carried enough whip for the two of them. And there was never any sliding around her, as much as I tried.

I worked at odd jobs from the time I was ten. Dragging hoses in the summer for a family friend who whitewashed barns, selling Christmas cards in the winter door-to-door, dipping ice cream at a nearby soda shop . . . it seemed I was always following in my parents' industrious footsteps. A dollar here, a dollar there, added up to two and soon a new baseball mitt or a used tennis racket, once I'd put enough away for the church plate and school lunch.

When I was a fresh teenager, just thirteen, I bought a newspaper route. I borrowed the money from the bank, paid seven dollars for each customer, 130 of them in all. I then paid the local newspaper to drop off that many papers each afternoon and I would deliver them, collect for them every other week, and pay the bank back each month. It was a terrific learning process, one that taught me banking and saving and accountability and retrieval and deadbeats, and it eventually allowed me to put enough away to help pay for part of my first year in college.

One gray, snowbound afternoon, as several of us waited for our papers at the usual drop, an older, more experienced boy offered me a puff of his cigarette. It was my first and I don't remember feeling one way or the other about it, except a bit guilty. I took several drags, picked up my papers, and went about delivering my route. It was a heavy, wet snow, and by the time I was finished, I was iced to the skin. As I entered the house at the basement door, I yelled up the short flight of stairs to the kitchen that I was home. I could smell dinner cooking. She, on the other hand, could smell something else.

"You've been smoking!" came the furious cry downward. Somehow, even after the long time away, she had picked up the scent. Somehow I would pay. She was protective and determined her sons would grow up decent and good. And even though she herself smoked in those days, she knew it wasn't right for me. Whether she told my father, who wasn't home from work yet, I never knew. But I do know I waited another five or six years before having another puff. And I made sure she was in another state.

Their life was tough, day to day, week to week, paycheck to paycheck, and they often took it close to the edge of a fiscal and emotional abyss. But somehow, always, that precipice remained a good cry away.

A good cry . . . or a bad one.

In the early fifties, we packed up everything and moved north to a tiny college town called Edinboro, hoping for some kind of luck.

They bought a fifteen-acre plot of ragged farmland outside of town, on which stood seven apple trees, four maples, an outhouse, a garage, and a rickety old two-story gray-shingled house. My mother and father had this idea of building cottages on the adjacent land and selling them to the servicemen returning from the Korean War. They both had come from well-bunkered families who would never have once given thought to taking such a chance. But it was a combination of their unique dreams and their financial desperation that sparked such a decision by my parents, one that ultimately and, like most other efforts, dismally failed.

"Our timing," my mother recalls, shaking her head, "was never very good."

Just as the first of what was figured to be many such one-bedroom, one-bath units was under way with money borrowed from my mother's mother, the government decided to cut back on the amount of housing aid it gave returning Korean vets who were headed back to school. Thus their grand scheme for "cottages" became a single "motel." And another dream had imploded. Dad found work again as a welder at a factory a half hour north in Erie, and Mom dug in working here, there, everywhere at once, it seemed.

And so life remained a day-to-day adventure. My brother and I, in the first decade of our lives, never realized how desperate times were. The neighbors across the street had a tiny black-and-white television, a marvelous new invention, which they shared with us in the afternoons after school. And when the days were long and sunny, we played in the apple orchard out back, the old outhouse turned on its side and made into a fort. There were exactly seven trees in that orchard, and while they bore some green, some red fruit, they bore sweeter dreams. Their gnarled limbs were perfect for climbing onto the stagecoach and off the castle and over the cliff, from one horse to another, one ship to the next. We were cowboys and Indians, Tarzan, pirates, French Legionnaires, living out whatever fantasy we might have seen on that small TV screen or at the twenty-five-cent Saturday doubleheader matinee.

There were no other children in the neighborhood my age so I became John Wayne, Errol Flynn, Wild Bill Hickok . . . always the hero saving the day. And when I tired of that, I moved to the old garage, got my baseball mitt and an old shriveled baseball wrapped in duct tape, and played ricochet well into the sunset. Off the roof, the drive to deep center field, back, back, back goes Kiner and he makes the diving catch to save Game Seven! A hot shot into the hole between second and short, Reese glides to his right, makes the back-handed stab, whirls and throws out the runner at first to preserve the no-hitter! We lived each day of our lives there in another world, either saving princesses or World Series, it didn't matter much which.

And so, while our parents were walking poverty's high-wire balancing act, we were innocently building our dreamland résumés, totally unaware there were problems.

One particularly bleak Christmas, when they both were working two jobs to no great avail, when they had hand-made many of our gifts and then mortgaged themselves for the rest, my brother and I saw to it that it would become their most unforgettable holiday ever.

It was my doing, for I was eight and he was four, and thus I was clearly in charge.

"Chuck!" I rustled him out of his tiny bed in the wee small hours of that morning. "I think I just heard Santa Claus. C'mon, let's go see!"

He and I crept quietly down the rickety back stairs of the old house, the wind blowing the night's snow hard against the windows. It was four A.M., the time of the devil in us.

We turned the corner and spotted the gifts beneath the tree in the living room. They hadn't been there the night before. *So there is a*

Santa Claus! I had reached the age of wavering, had heard the schoolyard tales. I was somewhere between desperately wanting to believe and desperately wanting to grow up. And this was my last Christmas on that fence. With that, we tore into the presents, ripping off the precious paper, reveling in our discoveries.

We had been about our business for nearly a half hour when, suddenly, we heard the gasps behind us and turned to see our weary parents standing at the door, one angry, the other in the beginning stages of a crying jag that would last a full day. It was years before either of us understood their uncontrollable sadness. They had worked in mills and nursing homes, plants and dairy bars, stores and beauty salons to simply break even, hold their heads above water. And they had gone beyond their means to try to make Christmas a happy moment in an otherwise dismal season. *Oh, to see the boys' eyes light up on that magic morning. Won't it be worth it?*

Instead, my brother and I saw in their eyes one of life's most profound and disturbing lessons. To this day, my mother remembers it happening but in another town, another place, another time. My father never spoke of it again.

We never had much except an ability to dream, to drift off somewhere else for a while. As a family, in pairs, or all alone on the limb of a crooked tree, we learned early that it was a wonderful method of transportation. Mom and Dad bought huge maps and planned outrageous trips, never taken. To Switzerland to visit his ancestors. To England to visit hers. On great airplanes and luxurious cruise lines. But a few hours east to see the changing leaves or an all-day journey to an aunt's farm was as glamorous as it ever got for us. The dreams, however, kept us all going. There was nothing better than that day every six months when the Sears and Roebuck catalog arrived. We called it "the Dream Book" and we would sit on the couch for hours, with all the money in the world, making our choices.

"I'd like that dress," she'd say, "in forest green."

"Could I get the cowboy boots?"

"That washing machine! Oh, wouldn't that be nice?"

"Only if I get the band saw too."

They would occasionally order the bare necessities from the Dream Book, school clothes, a tool or two, nothing much, but that book became as dog-eared as the family Bible over time, read and reread until the next one finally arrived.

Dreaming, by day and by night, was our escape.

And in the end, it would be his.

chapter three

walking to heaven

They were strong Christians, committed church people, there whenever the doors opened, always involved, no matter the number of times we packed up the rattletrap and moved up the road. Almost before they would find a new house, they would seek out a church, Presbyterian, Lutheran, Methodist . . . didn't seem to matter much as long as God lived there. My folks began as Lutherans, having grown up in that faith, but when there was no Lutheran church at their first stop away from their hometown, they simply found the best alternative—an active little Presbyterian community—and they kept that membership through three more towns until a small innerchurch uprising sent them across town to the Methodists.

It was never about the doctrine, never a definitive line between what the Lutherans believed as opposed to the Presbyterians, the Methodists, or even the Catholics. It was always, always, about God and their relationship with Him. And it had as much to do with what they gave back as with what they got. They were never merely casual parishioners, and as a consequence, neither were we.

With my brother and me firmly in tow, they became involved at every stop, which meant Sunday mornings, Sunday nights, Wednesday nights, and whenever else the organ sounded. Before long, with the signatures still damp on the letter of transfer from our previous church, she would be presiding over the women's ministry of the church and he would be serving as a deacon. We quickly became so much a part of the church that it might have seemed to others that we were born into it instead of freshly minted outsiders. Preachers and their families became our best friends. Even now at Christmas, cards from former pastors come from a dozen different directions, the Hogenbooms, Mayos, Griles, Koehlers, Prestons, reminders of lives gone by. It was simply the way my parents were raised.

My parents grew up in the same church, my mother almost literally, for her father was the caretaker of that lone Lutheran church in a small suburb of Pittsburgh and her mother helped take care of the manse. Appropriately, it was where my mother and father met and fell in love; she was a beautiful little redhead, he, the older, more mature boy from up the hill. He was nine and she was six when they first locked eyes in Sunday school.

"He was chubby and had on knickers and a beanie cap," she remembers fondly. "I went home and told my mother he looked like Fatty Arbuckle."

It wasn't love at first sight—hardly, at that age. But something registered and they began going to church functions together. Though she claims he always thought of her as "some little kid," there was something about her that kept him coming around. They actually began dating when she was fourteen, and they never went out with anyone else for the next six decades.

"We danced a lot," she says now. "I wasn't very good at it but he was. We just enjoyed being with each other so much."

He was a bit of an introvert in the early days, taking his refuge in the trumpet he played in the school band and in the bright-eyed redhead who was growing to love him.

Thus, the church was their meeting place and the cement that paved their way through the next sixty years together. It was the center of their lives and the sustenance of his dying days.

■ AUGUST 1999

In the beginning of the end, he walked to heaven.

It wasn't far—just from here to there—from the bedroom door down the short hallway of their tiny apartment. He had used his aluminum walker, inching his way to paradise.

"I was walking to heaven," he remembered vividly the next morning, the liver disease tinting his perpetual tan a sickly green.

"I don't know how I knew that was where I was going, but I'm sure it was. It was kind of misty. But when I got there, I heard this woman's voice tell me that it wasn't time. 'Go back,' she said. And so I was turning around when I heard another woman's voice."

That one was my mother's, calling from somewhere on the other side of sleep.

"Where are you going?" she asked. It was the middle of the night and the most obvious destination (two or three times a night at this point) was located next to the bedroom. This was a bit off the beaten path. He had never sleepwalked before, but a lot about him was changing, seemingly by the minute.

He had rarely remembered his dreams before the sickness came. But with it, they became vivid and stark—and often revealing. Road maps of the mind and soul.

"I was walking to heaven," he answered, confused and a bit amused. "I don't think it's time yet."

He thought about that dream for days, reveling in the memory, living it over and over and over again. At one point, he decided he recognized the voice that turned him back.

"You know," he mused, "I think it was her mother's voice." He motioned over his shoulder to my mother, who was busy in the kitchen.

"You think Grandma sent you back?" I asked. He just shrugged his shoulders and chuckled, feeling rather silly at the thought. My grandmother had been a large part of our lives, from the early days when she helped raise me, to the later years when she lived with us. It wasn't always easy, having your mother (and your mother-in-law and your grandmother) living under the same roof, sleeping in the bedroom right next to yours. The fact that my parents had had to occasionally rely on Grandma for their daily bread over the decades made it that much worse. I don't think it was overt, but she never let them forget it, either.

If she did indeed become the voice of heaven, as my father's dream suggested, then she found a voice in death that she had lost in her final days of life. She had always been the neatest, cleanest woman I have ever known, so particular that she could eat fried chicken with a knife and fork and clean every bone dry. She had the quickest of wits and was wonderful to be around. But as Alzheimer's (considered dementia in those days among nice people—craziness among the not-so-nice) set in, and she had to be moved into a rest home, she became quiet and lost, even angry at times. I had been so close to her when I was a child, had lived with her in our home through my high school years, and thus often turned to her for advice and aid. The shock of seeing her for the first time in the nursing home was something that will live with me forever. Her perfect white hair had become tangled and dull, her eyes glossy, and her time short. She spoke very little and in the end, if she knew who any of us were, she wasn't letting on. It was my first experience with the ravages of old age and I hated it, railed against it.

Almost to the exact day of her death twenty-four years later, at least in my father's dreams, she found her voice again. And—I'm imagining—that wonderful smile as well.

chapter four

hello, world

I've always felt awkward describing what it is I do for a living. To the Internal Revenue Service, I am a television sportscaster. My business card reads "essayist and commentator" but a very simple "storyteller" would work as well as anything, for that is what I do; I tell human stories. For decades, no matter the subject, if it needed a subtle, tender, sappy edge, it became my territory.

"Huberize it," the producer would explain, handing me an assignment that dealt with disabled or infirm people or worse.

"DiMaggio's dying. Huberize it."

"Found a Little Leaguer with no legs in Portland. Right up your alley."

It became almost an office joke. If there was tragedy involved, it most assuredly had my byline. How I came to this particular career crossroads is anybody's guess. I was born a reader, devouring everything that came within eyesight. As a child, in lieu of the morning newspaper, I read the cereal box, back, front, and sides, over and over again. I prized words and, later, the thoughts behind them. When I finally found that I could use them for a living, I took great joy in arranging them for the greatest impact, discovering I could have an effect on my reader, my listener, my viewer. Nothing pleased me more than a letter of emotional thanks for a reminder of life's priorities, or a brief but heartfelt tirade against my not-so-subtle tweaking. I got a hefty ration from both sides but, as one wise old boxing promoter told me, "Don't make no difference what they say, as long as they're saying it about you." They were watching and I was getting to them and it made me work even harder at the emotions behind the words.

"Dear Jerk," one unsigned viewer began, "give it up. You're the worst!"

"Dear Jim," the next letter read, "you make my day."

I never had much trouble keeping my ego balanced, for they often arrived in pairs like that. As though somehow coordinated, they always managed to keep my work in its proper perspective. Never too good, never too bad—sort of like Goldilocks's third bowl of porridge. At least, that was what I hoped. And as time passed and my hair grayed, I was allowed the luxury of the essay, a short, thoughtful sidebar to the main event, a breath in the midst of the breathtaking action. But in the main, for years, I simply told stories of the human condition.

It wasn't always the most pleasant of beats, to be sure, but it made good use of whatever gifts God had lent me. He offered me an ability to feel the pain, sense the turmoil, ask the proper questions, and package all of that in a way that I hoped became neither maudlin nor morose. That was always my goal from the time I began a project till I put a period on it at the end. Audiences rarely get the credit they deserve for having their own sense of balance and intuition. I didn't need to force their tears, their delight, or their anger; the viewers were altogether capable of that by themselves. But in that process, as

I tried to put a governor on my writing and offer some balance, I began to store the overload deep within myself.

There is no way to measure someone's emotional depth, no dipstick that comes up "half full" or "bottomless." But as I became the bearer of such heavy sentimental baggage, any casual check would probably have registered, "Stop! He's gonna blow!" As it turned out, it was this work that became my private armor. I had dealt with life's hazards and death's call for years, and when it finally came to my own family's doorstep, I at least knew the questions to ask.

"How do you feel?"

"What are the emotions flowing through you?"

"Are you frightened of death?"

"Where are you going from here?"

"Tell me about your dreams."

I had already asked these of strangers, adult and child alike, for years. At least I had the language down when it came time to ask the same of my father.

If I had suspected my own penchant for melodramatics during my ten years as a newspaperman, I likely could have carved myself quite a niche in the obituary department instead of sports. But that turn toward the emotional came a few years after crossing media and joining the television world where I unwittingly developed a rapport with the burdened, where tears seemed to naturally flow, both the subject's and mine. It was never like the crass character in the movie *Broadcast News* who forces a tear for the camera to somehow show his "compassion." My tears came against my will, bubbling over like some strange and salty brew. I tried to never show that side on camera, to never allow my own emotions to become a part of the story, except through my writing. (The weeks following my father's death did produce a particularly painful moment . . . but we'll save that for later.)

Blessedly, the powers that be allowed me my poetic freedom, to talk about an animal's mind or a child's soul, to take my stories beyond the usual blather that television can proffer. To be honest, I never knew why they allowed me that great latitude, gave me the luxury of sliding just beyond journalism's carefully structured boundaries into a poetic world where very few other broadcasters work, but I was humbled by their silence when it came time for a script to be okayed. Very often, they just handed it back and said, "Go make it sing."

In the early days it was simply what I did, how I worked, stuffed in among the daily, weekly, monthly hits, runs, and errors, but it blossomed into a regular show early in the '90s. Bill MacPhail, the wizened old man who invented instant replay and football blimp shots and created a television institution at the Masters while at CBS, was the original caretaker for CNN's sports coverage. He hired me in 1984 to coanchor the nightly highlight shows, and after a couple of years when that wore out, he tried me in nearly every time slot available. Weekdays, weekends, early mornings, late nights, overnights . . . didn't matter, let's see what works. Commentaries, two-minute sportscasts—they even came to me when CNN International took flight and asked me to do an international half-hour sports show every day.

"Me? I know nothing about those sports."

"Just until we find somebody who knows what he's talking about," they kidded. At least I thought at the time they were teasing. After the first month, I was certain they weren't.

"Hello, World" was my salutation . . . and it went downhill from there. I wasn't doing baseball or football or basketball or even hockey. I was doing soccer and cricket, rugby and snooker. The names were unpronounceable, the action indescribable.

We had one young producer from Wales working with us. He took me into an edit room one day and made me watch tapes of cricket matches for hours. "Just to get the lingo and see what they're doing," he said. I could understand neither.

The soccer (or football, as I learned to call it) was easier to comprehend than cricket, but we carried highlights from England, Scotland, Argentina, Australia—everywhere but America—and it became so muddled, I was completely lost. Every player had just one name; every team had two or three names; the crowds bordered on lunacy; the scores were low; I had trouble identifying.

And the language!

"And Manchester United wins it, two-nothing," I said on my very first show.

"No, nil! It's nil. Two-nil," the Welsh producer muttered in my ear. "Remember, we talked about that. They don't say 'zero' or 'nothing' in relation to scores. They say 'nil.'"

Of course. *Nil.* Made sense, I guessed (until I returned to the American airwaves and reported that "the Braves beat the Reds, 5-nil" and you should have seen the phones light up! "What's a *nil*?" "How much is a nil worth?" "Is that a two or a three in CNN language?").

So my international career was labored, at best. I worked at it and got a bit better until the real help blessedly came to the rescue—men from the BBC who knew what *nil* was worth. In fact, I enjoyed my time on the international desk, a respite from the mundane, learning fresh, new sports. And I enjoyed the mail. Every day's delivery brought a new adventure, stamped from a dozen different countries. I received a fair amount from Africa, oddly enough from young boys asking for help raising money for college. Ah, America, the land of the wealthy. You've just come into my house, they think, so you must be my new friend. Help me, friend.

But the best, most succinct note that seemed to sum up my international career came one day from Germany.

Dear Mr. Huber,

I enjoy your style but it's quite obvious you know nothing about our football. Congratulations on the façade.

My father didn't get to see any of this, fortunately, since it was telecast only outside of the United States. But we talked often and I told him of my blunders.

"It's okay," he comforted me, "but I wonder if any of my relatives in Switzerland have seen you?"

Hopefully . . . not.

It lasted only six tormented months, and then I was sent back to the network's domestic front lines in search of my real calling.

The only thing we didn't try over the years of searching was chalk talks, and I was thinking that would be next when Bill MacPhail called me into his office in the late days of 1991. Either that or a promotion to Dubuque.

"I'm at a loss," he said. He prided himself not only on being an industry innovator, but also on having a keen eye for talent. Name any of the best network sportscasters over the '50s, '60s, and '70s, and chances are, MacPhail had hired them. If he hadn't believed so strongly in his own gut instinct about people, chances are, I would've been on the streets long before then. Perhaps interviewing for the obit job. It wasn't that I was horrible; it was simply that I wasn't very good where I was. But he wasn't giving up . . . not yet.

"I can't figure it out. We've tried you everywhere. I know you can write. I know you can tell stories. I'm not real keen on your basketball highlights, mind you, but I just know there's something that's perfect for you here. What is it? Where do we go? You have any ideas?"

I was moving in my chair as he talked, ready with an answer before the question ever came. If he was frustrated, I was more so. I had grown to detest anchoring highlight shows and it probably showed. If I had to describe one more slam dunk, one more "deep, deep, deep to right-center field," one more leaping touchdown catch, I was going to enter the priesthood. (But don't tell my mother that; she'd have gladly taken me up on the idea!)

For the first two years at the network, after moving across town from local television, I had coanchored the 11:00 P.M. show, done a midnight cut-in, and soloed the 2:30 A.M. show for the West Coast audience. An hour and five minutes, total, of fast-paced scores and highlights every night. I was a writer, a journalist, and yet there seemed little time for that. On a normal winter's night, for instance, there might have been a dozen NBA games, a dozen more NHL games, twice as many college basketball games—not to mention the news from the boardrooms, jailhouses, and mortuaries. There was even one particular weekend—just one—every fall when every single sport known to mankind was in business. Try to fit all *that* into a half hour and be creative at the same time! It doesn't work unless you want to be cute or funny . . . and I was hardly either. So I fired away, trying to build as much emotion and feeling as I could but, in the process, becoming a bore, both to myself and *surely* to the audience. It wasn't me, for sure.

The hours were grueling. I would leave for the network early in the afternoon and get home at 3:30 A.M. Neighbors were wondering why I was collecting the morning paper in my bathrobe at noon each day. My son was wondering why Dad was always asleep when the school bus came and gone when the bus came back. Finally after two years on that schedule, I went to MacPhail and asked for a change.

"What took you so long?" he asked with a smile. "We've all been wondering when you would cave in."

It wasn't the hours as much as the sameness. Everything had started to look alike, every home run, every diving catch, every wraparound goal. When I found myself screaming at the camera, which I swore to myself I would never do when I reluctantly entered the TV business, I knew the end had to be near. If there was ever, and continues to be, something that grinds at my nerves, it's a sportscaster who feels that he has to yell at the audience to be heard. The listener is in control of the volume and, in the end, the channel changer.

Far too many of the young sportscasters develop their styles in caricature, taking the worst traits of those they emulate and building upon them. Sports reporting is certainly not a matter of life and death—at least most nights. But it isn't *Saturday Night Live,* either. Obviously, that is simply my take, for there are many who have taken such acts to national prominence. It's just a personal preference. When I watch a sports highlights show, I want the scores, the highlights, and some pertinent information. I don't want vaudeville. The problem with my view is that so much competition exists in the cable industry—network after network offering the same scores, same highlights, same stories, same information—you need "an act" to separate yourself from the rest. I didn't have one . . . at least not yet.

Oddly enough, the corners of MacPhail's office were piled high with résumé tapes from eager young men and women who would've given their entire year's allowances to do what I was hating. I often wondered what in the world was wrong with me—and I'm sure they would have wondered too. But I knew exactly what I wanted to do and how I wanted to do it. I had mentioned the idea several times in years gone by and received a shrug and a "We'll think about it," which they never did. Now I had my opening.

"Gimme five minutes, Bill," I quickly told him, "and I'll have a proposal on your desk."

Five minutes later—probably less—I knocked on his door and handed him a short outline for a show that would become known as *The Sporting Life,* a series of stories about people who challenged the odds, who somehow took life's lemons and opened a lemonade stand. They were everywhere and their tales weren't being told with the depth and emotion that they deserved. In my bottom drawer were several large files of potential stories, ideas I had been stockpiling on and off for several years. This would be the perfect forum, for them *and* for me. I would have my own producer and camera crew, and I would travel, telling stories.

"Why haven't you brought this up before?" he said with a chuckle, his memory far better than it would be in years to come. "Let me take this to the powers that be and I'll have an answer for you this week. I think this could be what we're both needing here."

In three days, we got the okay, minus the "crew." I was given a producer and whatever cameraman was available at the time. That would be the pattern for the entire run of the show. Truth be told, they could have skimped on the producer and bulked up on the crew, but I was willing to take anything and anybody. And it changed my life forever.

It was a forum, in the best sense of the word, one I jealously guarded and took great pains in protecting. Did I ever abuse the privilege? Not consciously, ever. But I'm certain I used it, often, to further causes, bring awareness to the world's eye. To sell hope, love, pain, honor, justice . . . and an occasional fruitcake.

Cancer, leukemia, blindness, MS, autism, AIDS, drug abuse, old age, homelessness, bus and car and horse crashes . . . victims of all of these became part of my "family." Eight lives, including a thirty-year-old racehorse and a ninety-five-year-old coach, ended in the months and years after we told their stories, leaving me with a gnawing void. I grieved for each of them as they went. The dipstick rapidly read "overflowing," but it became a kind of sentimental boot camp that would unknowingly prepare me for the personal journey on which I would embark in the years to come.

Every moment I spent with my father during those final fifteen months, I drew from my experiences with *The Sporting Life*. I had been with families who had lost their children, children who had lost their parents. I had sat and heard their stories and cried with them. Armor, then, for my own personal battle. Or so I thought at first.

chapter five

a man of many degrees

Prophetically, because she taught me so much about living and dying, our very first subject set the standard for a decade of *Sporting Life* shows.

Heather Farr, a wisp of an Arizonan, had battled breast cancer and seemingly had beaten it. She was ready to make her way back to the Ladies Professional Golf Association tour. We spent five days documenting her story for that debut show, an inordinate amount of time in those days. In the months and years to come, we often were restricted (by budget and time) to only a few hours with a subject to document the tale. Fly in, do the interview, shoot some b-roll, and fly home again. It never seemed like enough time to do the job right. There was always one more box of old photographs to shoot, one more game for a different angle, one trip to the cemetery, the courthouse, the doctor's office, that would be left for another time, if ever. But because we had set the debut of the show several months away, we were afforded the luxury of time for this story. And a week in Phoenix with our subject and her family.

We went to the driving range with Heather, sitting at her feet as she hit ball after ball, followed her to the equipment factory where she was being refitted for the clubs she would use on her comeback trail. We went home with her as she pruned her beloved roses and to her family's home for spaghetti the night before we left.

Heather Farr was a fighter. The cancer that had eaten away at her probably would have quickly consumed a lesser soul. But through fierce determination and a will much larger than her tiny frame, she was able to smile at last and point to a day not far down the road when she would return to tournament golf.

"I'm going to come back," she told me. "You just watch. I'm going to make it."

And there was no arguing that.

Returning to the studio, I set about the tedium of logging all of the twenty videotapes we shot (obviously, another part of the routine that was quickly trimmed). In the years to come, we would not only spend less time shooting, but also shoot far, far fewer tapes. Somehow it always seemed to work out, though that's hardly the way to do a documentary show. Twenty tapes was our high number, a single hour-long tape our low.

"Make do" was our credo. "Make do, and make it sing."

My time alone in an edit suite with the tapes has always been a part of the writing process, to log each second of video, to know exactly what I have to work with, to experience the subject one last time before sitting down to write. In the case of Heather Farr, that simply drove the emotional nails deeper. Sitting in the dark, the video reflecting in my tears, I found from the very outset that this was going to be a unique and often-overwhelming exercise. The interview itself had been difficult, so emotional for both of us. But to be alone in that edit room, running the tape back again and again, her words echoing like trumpets in a hallway, I found new feelings coursing through my veins. I would freeze the picture, stare into her eyes, and see deep within her soul. How could someone this young and this fragile fight such a battle as this? From whence does such courage come? I reveled at her story and, a bit selfishly, knew that she would be absolutely perfect in the leadoff role for this new show.

Heather and I became close friends in the months that followed, and whenever I was in Phoenix on business, we would have dinner or at least make contact. Our phone conversations often ranged deep into the night. She seemed to sense a kindred spirit and shared her brightest hopes and darkest fears. She invited us to return for her wedding a year after our first story ran. A dozen ex-suitors sprinkled throughout the jammed cathedral to watch a magnificent bride take her vows, tears streaming down her cheeks, for it hadn't been that long ago that she thought she would never, ever see this day.

And eight months later, we came back to the very same chapel to document her funeral. The cancer had returned with a vengeance, ravaging her small body until there was hardly anything left. For all of her toughness, she was simply worn down. Her death hit all of her friends and family hard. But for some odd reason, it touched me far deeper than I would have ever suspected. She was the first of eight subjects from our show to die, the grand marshal of a sad parade. And though each reached deep inside me to clutch at my soul, she set the tone.

I have had my tussles with God over the years but rarely did I ever question a decision any more vehemently than this one. With all of the ugliness mankind has created, how could He steal a young beacon of hope and courage and bravery? I wasn't as angry as I was deeply mystified over such a choice. But it's a question all children ask, no matter their age. And it would be one I would ask again, a decade later, for more personal reasons.

When we ask, "Why?" we rarely expect an answer . . . or at least not one that makes much sense. But in the case of Heather Farr, perhaps it simply took a lot longer than most. Why did she die? What purpose did it serve? It saved her younger sister's life—*that's* what purpose her death served.

Missy Farr had been a great amateur golfer in her own right and dreamed of joining her sister on the LPGA tour, but she gradually moved out of Heather's shadow and into a different direction. She had a son who was one of the brightest lights in the darkness that would envelop Heather's final days.

Two years after Heather died, Missy was diagnosed with breast cancer. For a family that had no history of cancer on either side, this was far beyond coincidence. Could it have been the chemicals sprayed on golf courses? Could it have been the power plant near where the two sisters spent so much time as children learning how to play golf? There are no answers to this particular "why." But because cancer had become such an enormous part of the Farr family for the past few years, the awareness took Missy to a doctor at a very early stage.

"Her cancer," says Sharon Farr, who would have fought the devil bare-handed to save either of her daughters, "was just as angry, just as bad, as Heather's. But we caught it early and that made all the difference in the world.

"Heather saved her sister's life, in other words, from the grave."

There are foundations across the world established to fight breast cancer, to find a cure. The Heather Farr Foundation is the symbol, instead, of awareness, just as she herself was in the end. And because Heather herself climbed the monumental mountain range of insurance problems during her last year or two, the foundation allows those victims of breast cancer who don't have insurance to still get whatever medical help they need.

"There are too many women dying who don't have to," says Sharon Farr.

Her oldest daughter was one of them.

Did my encounters along the way line me with asbestos, to better absorb the fires of death? There were times when I wanted to believe that and times when the lining was mere tissue paper, the flames seeming to eat away at my insides until I was raw and unable to handle much more.

Are we ever prepared? Is a mortician or minister better equipped? Does rubbing the shoulders of infirm people on a weekly basis help or hurt? How do you insulate yourself—or should you?

I did not start out to be a sportscaster, but once I had settled into that area of the media, I felt shielded from the world's problems. After all, for all of its drama, this wasn't war and it wasn't brain surgery. But as I traveled the roads through the next thirty years, as a newspaper sportswriter and then a radio sportscaster before turning to television, I found the blending immeasurable. It often *was* war, *was* brain surgery. There were times when I felt I needed degrees in law, medicine, art, history, psychology, political science, just to intelligently cover one team for one season.

The quarterback sues to break his contract and we must know precisely the terminology to tell both sides of his story and often decide for ourselves who is right and who is wrong. The right guard strains his anterior cruciate ligament and we talk to doctors and discover new methods of surgery and rehabilitation. The aesthetics of the new arena lean toward a Frank Lloyd Wright dimension and we must know that the angles will not always be pleasant or square. The league floundered during the Great Depression and disbanded during World War II but roared back into prosperity in the postwar era and we must know where and why. The coach sits the starting center on the bench for a quarter, letting him watch the sub who doesn't have as much talent but who works harder, and we watch the amazing transformation and learn that it is an old and honored art. The new stadium won't get built without taxpayer approval of a floating bond issue and we delve into the inner workings of those whom we elect. Law, medicine, art, history, psychology, political science—all in the same season.

And that college counselor who suggested majoring in English? Well, there's that too. You do have to know how to put all of those subjects into a good, understandable sentence. But if English is good, how about French? So many of the hockey players I worked with over the years barely spoke English. And now, the NHL is such an amalgamation of nations that you almost need to understand and speak a dozen different languages to do your job. So you must be adaptable and expandable in the sportswriting and sportscasting business.

When I turned to the subtleties of *The Sporting Life*, with all of its pain and hope, perhaps a double major in religion and philosophy might have been worthwhile as well, for they often entered the mix.

An old playground basketball legend needs a heart transplant. A former pro football Hall of Famer, father of eight, is defrauded of his entire life savings. One of the young swimmers survives the deadly Notre Dame bus wreck. The baseball Hall of Famer must bury not one, but two wives. The one-legged golfer teaches the game to people who are blind and disabled. The deaf football team and the homeless cricket players and the high school kids take disabled folks on hunting trips.

Tell me the sporting life is just hits, runs, and errors. Tell me it is not the world in microcosm. Tell me it doesn't tear at your very soul. My *Sporting Life* certainly did.

chapter six

death comes knocking

■ SEPTEMBER 18, 1999

"Come quickly," my mother called early on a Monday morning in late September.

I was in Boston. It was the day after the 1999 Ryder Cup. We were going to take a few hours to tour the city, to wash away the grueling drama and bitter aftertaste left over from the weekend. It had been a remarkable comeback by the Americans but the ugliness of the galleries and the controversial scene on the seventeenth green did what some feel might be irreparable harm to the game. The age-old grace and serenity became lost in a jubilant melee by the United States team, rushing onto the green after Justin Leonard had made a cross-country putt to win his match and decide the event. It left a bitter taste in the Europeans' mouths and became headline fodder for every traditionalist worldwide. I was glad it was over and needed a breath of fresh air. I would get none for the next

---

three weeks. In fact, I took hardly a breath at all. A suffocating standoff had begun.

"The dying process has started and we need you," my mother said in a measured tone. "I don't think he has much time left at all. Please hurry."

It was not the beginning of the hysteria. For the past fifteen months, we had been existing on the edge, sure that he would die tomorrow. The doctor's theory of "less than a year, more than a month" was only half right. Apparently, he hadn't measured the man's will.

My brother and his family lived in the same Maryland town where my parents had chosen assisted-living after a lifetime in Pennsylvania and Florida. I lived in Atlanta, eighty minutes away by plane, eleven hours by car . . . no time at all by heart.

"I wouldn't trade places with you for anything," Chuck told me one night in the final weeks, probably trying to assuage my guilt at being away so much, unable to physically help. He and his family had been on call twenty-four hours a day, rushing Dad to the emergency room, helping Mom when he fell, enduring his turmoil and her emotional pain—caregivers of the first order.

"You, far away, not knowing . . . and also not able to take advantage of every possible moment with him."

And frightened of death, I, too, had no envy.

We were both novices at this dying thing, handling it as brothers might, in our own personal ways.

My wife's father died of a sudden heart attack at fifty, her mother of a lingering, agonizing cancer ten years later. Chuck's wife had lost her mother similarly. Their experiences became sturdy canes, helping us walk those final days somehow, although there came a time when "oh, that's very normal in situations like this" made us both entertain the darkest of husbandly thoughts.

"For heaven's sake, what is normal about this?"

Nothing. And everything.

My brother and I had drifted apart in the years after high school. We seemed to have little in common but blood. While I was into sports and dating and school politics, he was quiet, immersing himself in his music and his books. The four years that separated us truly did that, separated us. It wasn't until he married for the second time and his bride decided to play family "matchmaker" that we began drifting close again. She worked hard at it, getting us together on a semi-regular basis, making sure we talked on the phone and exchanged cards. It was a selfless, wonderful gesture that finally brought us to a warm relationship neither of us ever expected or intended.

In fact, her diligence and fervor expanded my own world considerably. I had always been fairly adept at drawing, doodling from my earliest recollection. As an adult, what I drew or painted stayed at home, hung in a bathroom or the guest room, hidden away from most eyes. I did mostly faces, people in situations, children at play, old men on a park bench; but to me, they were crude and amateurish (and rightfully so, wouldn't you think?). But one Thanksgiving, Chuck and Pam visited, staying in that guest room, and when they left, we discovered two empty spots on the wall. They had slipped two paintings into their luggage and taken them home to a favorite gallery. They showed my work to the owner and somehow talked him into hosting a one-man exhibition. He surely liked the idea of featuring a television personality far more than he admired the paintings themselves; I'm convinced of that. There was one small problem: he needed at least twenty more pieces to fill his walls. And so, still shocked at the idea but committed, I set about the business of painting, sheltering myself in the upstairs studio for hours and days until I had put together enough to fill out the gallery's walls. It probably wasn't the way Van Gogh went about his art and you wouldn't have caught Rembrandt in such mass production, but I was neither . . . nor did I ever pretend to be. We held the show, sold a few paintings, built my ego to the point where I thought I was now a working artist, and I came back to Atlanta with great stars in my eyes.

We held several more one-man exhibitions, sold three or four more pieces, gave a few more away to restaurants and hotels, but there were still dozens remaining . . . far too many for either the bathrooms or the guest room. So I found my own gallery not far from home, a wonderful little co-op with nothing but local artists—mostly women—who took me in like a child from a storm. They weren't sports fans by any stretch, but somehow took the idea of having a "TV person" in their midst as something special. And there, on one wall, facing colorful geraniums or a peaceful mountain stream, hangs my work today: a delirious hippie from Belize, an old woman in a snowstorm, a jubilant Olympic champion, a little boy hefting a basketball, a smoking Arab, a woman in thought, Willie Mays . . . the people of my imagination and surroundings. They are all there thanks to one energized sister-in-law trying to make a family out of two grown men.

What they and their children went through on a daily, hourly basis during my father's final months was grandly heroic. They both worked miles away, he as a church business administrator, she as a secretary, and yet they often sacrificed their jobs and home lives for my parents' care. While I was able to help a bit financially, they gave the hands-on assistance. It was not a very fair trade-off in my eyes, but one that couldn't be helped.

The first summer of my dad's demise, in 1998, was as frightening and tumultuous as could be possible. To imagine just the two of them in a small, dark two-bedroom apartment, living in constant fear, sends shivers. Room 108 on the ground floor of the relatively inexpensive dwelling was far more brooding than I could have ever stood. Only two large windows—one in the living room, one in their bedroom—allowed in any light. And because the sun struck that particular side of the building throughout the day, they kept the blinds partially closed and so, even midday, it seemed overcast and sullen. It became almost a habit; as soon as I would arrive and make my round of hugs, I would edge toward the living room window and slide the blinds open, allowing the outside world in. And before long, subtly, my mother would make a point of tending to her plants and darken the room again. They took to it as they took to every place we ever lived, from quiet side street to busy highway to trailer park. In the years that I grew up, we lived in thirteen different homes, and they added four more after I was gone. They brightened them all with their love for each other, and that always seemed to be light enough.

Though my brother and his family were near in the final months, they could not spend every moment with my father and mother and so the loneliness and terror surely became overwhelming. Children huddled against the monster. Old people hearing death knocking at the door.

"June was the worst," my mother says now, slowly, quietly, drawing the words out to fit the thirty days.

As I look at the calendar she kept, the images burst forth from the black and white. A peaceful picture of an old naval sailing ship in the Baltimore harbor sits atop the records of a dying man. Five different doctors and as many theories and treatments. If he wasn't going to one of them, he was being rushed to an emergency room. Every night, she would faithfully update me, both on his welfare and their mutual heartbeat. From long distance, it sounded terrible. Up close, it was twice that.

June 1—Bob to doctor (codeine)
June 2—Bob's CAT scan (Demerol)
June 3—Bob to doctor (morphine)
June 4—to emergency room, spitting up blood
June 5—platelets given
June 8—vomiting blood, nosebleed

June 9—Bob to doctor, blood work, X rays

June 10—MRI on back and stomach, ultrasound on legs

June 11—Charlie delivers communion to the house

June 12—Bob to doctor

June 17—MRI

June 19—to emergency room (11 A.M.–6 P.M.)

June 23—Bob to doctor

June 24—Bob to doctor

June 26—to emergency room, possible stroke

June 27—MRI

They lived as they had for so long, on the very edge. But this time, on the edge of life itself. He might go for a week without the bleeding and then, suddenly, it came like a flood. Through it all, as they caught their breath, they would sit together, hold hands, and cry. That was nothing new, for their tears had mingled for years, but for other reasons.

When my father was finally forced to retire early from the post office because of spinal degenerative disease, he had to wait two years until his pension started. Two years with no income. They never once let on to either my brother or me, keeping their fears bundled deep inside. They were living in the mountains of North Carolina then. Often, as the darkness set in, they would put on one of their favorite gospel records, and as Bill Gaither's voice filled the room with hope, they sat and cried together.

But those were worldly tears, as it were—tears of desperation. These, now, were altogether different.

"We just took it one day after another," my mother remembers. "We were hoping for more time together, begging for more time, but in the end, he was ready."

Hospice became involved, blessedly, in the spring of 1999, taking much of the pressure off my mother. The idea of his disease being fatal did not sink in until the eighteenth of May when his lead doctor made the decision to call in Hospice. It was blunt, but it was the best thing that could have happened. They were there, every day, to lift and support not only him, but her as well.

"Hospice" is an age-old idea, a resting place for travelers and pilgrims, still quite common in Europe. And even in its modern sense, it is still firmly rooted in ancient cultures. Years ago there were no hospitals, no rest homes, and so people often died at home, loved ones caring for them, making their final days as peaceful and pleasant as possible.

Hospice, with a capital *H*, is only a few decades old, formally begun in 1967 by a British physician named Cicely Saunders. Students at Yale University in America heard of her program in London that offered special care for people diagnosed with irreversible illnesses, and they invited Dr. Saunders to speak on their campus. She became a visiting faculty member of the Yale School of Nursing for the 1965 spring term. In the years to follow, the dean of that school, Florence Wald, went to work at Saunders's inpatient Hospice in London called St. Christopher's, learning everything she could about the idea, eventually bringing it home. In 1974, a Connecticut Hospice nurse and volunteer made their first home-care visit and one of the most humane revolutions in history had taken its American turn.

While most of the care is done in the patient's home, there are more and more Hospice facilities built every year, houses where those who have no family can spend their final days under the watchful and caring eyes of volunteers and trained nurses. In lieu of flowers when my father finally died, we asked for donations to the Hospice building fund. A peaceful fifteen-acre plot of land, exactly twenty-one miles from my parents' doorstep, was bestowed and plans drawn up. Though he would not have been eligible to stay there, Dad would have loved the view, the rolling mountainside off to the left beckoning one last drive to see the leaves change.

For every two full-time Hospice employees, there is one volunteer. Volunteers are some of the most special people on God's earth. They work, in the words of the World Health Organization's description, "to neither hasten nor postpone death, to provide pain relief and integrate the psychological and spiritual aspects of patient care and offer a support system to both help patients live as actively as possible and help the family cope during the illness and in their own bereavement."*

And so when the doctors saw that my father had little time, and yet did not need to be under the constant hospital watch, they called Hospice.

But Hospice is supposed to be for the last days. In 1999, the average length of Hospice stay was twenty-nine days. As late as 1990, there was a 210-day lifetime limitation under the Medicare Hospice benefit before it would be removed as a provision. My father would have used up three-quarters of that, astonishing them hourly, somehow clinging for months to his dignity and humor like a lifeline. The volunteers' days were filled with the stench of death at nearly every stop, but this patient seemed different for a good, long time. They looked forward to their hours with him, becoming first caretakers, then friends, and finally part of the family, spending far more time than was called for, sitting, talking, venting.

In a strange way, he nursed them as much as they did him, making them laugh, giving them a moment of brightness. How they managed day in and day out, dealing with the morbid task of preparing the dying, I will never know. Perhaps that one rare individual like my father helped offer some kind of balance. Often, I would pass a nurse in the hallway, coming from his room, shaking her head in amazement, chuckling.

---

* World Health Organization, 1999.

"Your dad . . . he's something very special. I hope you realize just how much so."

I hadn't, but I was learning.

If there can be good fortune in a situation such as this, he was blessed. There was little pain at all and he remained somewhat lucid nearly to the end, although the dreams seemed to sometimes paint him otherwise. It was as if, on occasion, he was unable to come fully awake, the dream continuing in the darkness of the bedroom, his eyes open but his mind still hard at work on some strange adventure. As death crept closer, the dreams became more panoramic and expressive, if for no one other than those standing by, watching the process. It became a light that allowed us to look a level or two within him, to join him on his way. Or perhaps, exhausted, it was his convoluted way of explaining what was happening. Dreams became a daily, hourly subject. As soon as he would awaken, much as a faithful psychiatrist's patient, he would dutifully tell his latest tale. He understood very little, could only relay, but seemed to relish the telling.

"The pickup truck," he would croak, "where's the pickup truck?"

"Huh?"

"The pickup truck was coming to get me," he would continue, almost irritated at our ignorance. I don't think he had ever ridden in one, let alone owned one, and yet pickup trucks seemed to drive through the dreams of his dying days. Why? Who can explain dreams? If they are the canvas of the subconscious, as some think, his paintbrush gave us vivid masterpieces those final weeks. Perhaps as the brain attempts to make some order out of the disarray, it uses dreams as a method of deep communication. He had someplace to go, and if he couldn't walk, a pickup truck would do. After all, his thin single bed would fit nicely in the back and a pickup truck matched his budget and his lifestyle, spare and durable.

"Have you ever thought of taking a limo?" I teased him once.

"It's much more comfortable than a pickup truck and so much more stylish."

He looked at me peculiarly and wrinkled his nose.

"Have the new cars come out yet?"

That magical moment each fall, like the arrival of the huge Sears catalog, was another time for family dreaming. The new lines would come to the corner showroom and we would make our choices, knowing such a wish would never be granted. Our cars were always used vehicles, but the idea of something brand-spanking new was an enticing carrot for the weary rabbit. And yet while he wanted to know about the new cars, he would have gladly spent the rest of his life behind the wheel of the four-year-old Buick that used to sit outside their apartment complex, their final chariot.

If you asked him to find a moment in time when death began, he would have probably pointed to the day just eleven months before when, after a few close calls (and Mom's inability to drive because of a nerve disorder in her feet), they decided to sell that last car. Death's approach was marked not by the transfusion decades before, not by the early symptoms—the strange bleeding, the headaches and dizziness—not even by the calling of Hospice. No, death began its countdown in his mind when they were relegated for the rest of their lives to someone else's backseat. Over the years, they had put more miles on a car than seemed possible, driving off to a craft show or the mountains or their sons' homes for the holidays. Dad took great delight in mapping his journeys, finding new shortcuts, discovering how the landscape had changed from one visit to the next. He had the kind of mind that absorbed the slightest detail, and once he'd made one successful trip, that route was etched forever.

"There used to be a gas station on the corner there," he would say.

"Now there's an office building. And have you seen that house with the huge columns right as you come around the bend on 441?"

I likely hadn't. Nor could I even recall where 441 was. I am a visual person, not a numbers guy.

"You ever take 23 coming down?" he would ask. "Oh, it's a breeze, and it avoids all that truck traffic. You oughta try it. See, it goes . . ." and almost before he'd unpacked the car, he would spend his first half hour out from behind the wheel dissecting his map.

When I would travel on my job, his atlas was never far from his side, plotting just exactly where I was. He never physically joined me on my journeys but was always there vicariously. Before my first golf vacation to Scotland, I bought him a map of the country so he could follow along in absentia. And when I returned, we bent carefully over it, retracing my steps. Here to Glasgow, then to Troon, on to Gullane . . .

It was, like his dreams, his escape.

I had an itch over those last fifteen months, probably prompted by some Hollywood theatrics or by Jim Dodson's wonderful book *Final Rounds*, of simply driving up to the apartment door one day, putting him in my car, taking him to Dulles Airport, and flying with him to Switzerland. To allow him to at last see his homeland in person, after all those years spent with books and movies and pictures. He talked about it often. His brother and family had made the trip, and though Dad never said so, he was jealous of their experience. There were relatives still living there (in Bern, he believed) and he could take out the atlas and quickly pinpoint that particular part of the world. I had the itch and never scratched it, something I will regret for the rest of my life. The doctors would have railed against it, my mother would have blanched, but it would have been worth the persecution. Dreams . . .

"Can't tell you how much I miss driving," he said. "Life just will never be the same again."

And it wasn't.

chapter seven

a long-distance calling

It isn't as though my parents disapproved of my profession; it was simply that they had always had other plans for their elder boy. At least my mother did. I don't recall my father ever having much of a say in it. She had wanted me to be a minister, and probably to make her happy, I began to wander down that road in the beginning. For a while, I truly believed it to be my calling, even to the point of imagining a visitation.

Perhaps it wasn't imagination. I was still in high school, being twisted and turned by the normal teenage cyclone. I was into sports, school politics, and dating, perhaps not in that order, but also seemed to be beckoned by a persistent religious muse.

One evening, I found myself alone in the darkened sanctuary of our church, the rest of the youth group long gone. I was sitting in a pew near the front; I'm not certain how I got there or even why. Perhaps I was trying to make something happen, for I knew how much my parents wanted me to become a pastor. I thought I wanted that as well, but it seemed like I was working awfully hard to make it "magically" happen. Wasn't God supposed to appear in the quiet night, take me in His arms, and show me the way? Wasn't that how it worked? And so I supposed if I created the atmosphere enough times, if I left myself open to His call, it would surely come. Whether it did or whether I simply imagined it, I cannot say. But that night, with the slender moon drifting through the large stained-glass window behind the choir loft, I saw a form, heard a voice, felt a tremor, and knew that my moment had arrived.

I remember breaking into tears, shivering uncontrollably, before slowly making my way out of the church to begin the short drive home. This was it; there wasn't any way around it now; I had been called to the pulpit. With all of my usual subtle bombast (for I was a bit of a dramatist as well), I let everyone know what had happened. I might as well have hung a huge banner across Main Street for, being a small town, the word spread quickly. My mother the bank teller helped, I'm guessing. There would be no question about my call now.

I earned a partial academic scholarship to a tiny Presbyterian college in South Carolina and enrolled as a pre-ministerial student, certain that it would provide the path for my future. My parents were so proud, their dreams for me (and for them) finally coming true. But when I decided to stray, I did a masterful job of it. My grades were shoddy, my work habits poor, and my thirst for the nightlife mighty. Though this was chiefly a men's college (there were six female students, most of them living in town and not on campus), there were five women's colleges within striking distance. And so it seemed that each night was made for another foray. I had never lived away from home, had never been out from under my parents' firm thumbs, and when I finally was, I was determined to make up for lost time.

On one of those evening "raids," I was introduced to Carol, the woman who would later become my wife, forever. I met her on a blind date, and I have a fraternity brother (who later became the minister of one of the largest Presbyterian churches in the South) to thank for it. With Carol now just twenty-six miles away by car, by thumb, by foot, or by bus, I had quickly put aside whatever words might have been whispered in that darkened sanctuary just a year or so before. School could wait. I was rapidly becoming a man and that seemed far more important. I was also becoming a fixture at her home, so much so that her mother worried more about my schoolwork than I did.

"You here again?" she would say with a laugh. "Did you bring your books?"

And, of course, I hadn't. They were heavy and the walk was hilly. If I couldn't catch a ride, I would hitchhike. And worst-case scenario, I walked. One night, her mother had seen me one too many evenings there and firmly suggested I hit the road. I did, but the road was empty and I wasn't up to the walk that night so I found a used-car lot and curled up in the backseat of the only car they'd left open. That morning, I sheepishly called Carol and told her what had happened. Her father, a traveling salesman, picked me up and drove me the twenty-six miles to school, suggesting I find alternative means of transportation in the future. And so I did, walking the next time down farm roads and up darkened hills, chased by dogs, hooted at by owls, arriving at dawn's first light; it was never the best route home. And of course, dead tired, I would sleep through my morning classes. It's a wonder they allowed me to even finish the school year.

Nothing much came out of that year except my love for Carol. My journalistic career could have gained a kick-start there, in fact, but I managed to circumvent that too. I was asked to join the campus newspaper staff, and since I had worked on the yearbook in high school, I figured it might be a snap. And when they handed me my first assignment, a basic rewrite, I fidgeted and fussed over it for so long I eventually wound up plagiarizing what they'd given me. It was, in all, not one of my finer seasons and I think often now of those men with whom I went to college. They see my name, hear my voice now, recognize my face, and wonder where in the world is the justice. The school itself, terribly offended at my academic and social behavior four decades ago, sends letters monthly now asking for donations. Once, in fact, they asked me to return to speak at a function but I found an excuse to decline. Imagine the chagrin, one of their most decorated alums (or so they contend) and the record he really left there.

Of course, memories grow very colorful in the wake of so-called celebrity. I had been on my high school basketball team, had played very poorly and thus sporadically, but when the occasion came years later for my old coach to introduce me as the night's speaker, I suddenly became the greatest player in his coaching history. I sheepishly reminded him of my nickname, given to me by him that season. "Giraffe" he called me, for I seemed all neck and legs and little talent.

My time at the Presbyterian college, such as it was, is a hodgepodge of memories, most I'm perfectly glad my father will never hear (at least until he reads this, as I'm certain he shall). I went to chapel, as we all were required, and seemed buoyed by the message, yet I strayed once outside the doors. I found jobs here and there to subsidize my meanderings. Several of us hired a local woman to make sandwiches for us every night and bag them up. We then made our rounds of the dormitories, selling them at an exaggerated price to the guys feverishly studying. (Of course, I was never one of the studiers . . . but we all have a purpose in life.)

I worked as a waiter at a small restaurant off campus and after a while became almost a surrogate son to the man and wife who owned the place. They seemed to sense the child in me they never had and kept me fed, made sure I had spending money, let me off when I needed the time, and even armed me.

The Thanksgiving holidays arrived and two classmates from Florida invited me to ride home with them. But the Cuban missile crisis was in full fury. Though my own parents in Florida never mentioned any threat, the owners of the restaurant somehow felt I was entering enemy territory. They could see, in their mind's eyes, an invasion that would begin in Key West and march northward, an inverse Sherman.

"You know," the man said to me, "you could get down there and they'll have invaded Florida and what are you gonna do? It's possible. They say the Cubans are ready and who's gonna stop them?"

And so, as I stood by the car readying for the six-hour drive, they handed me bundles of food, blankets, water, a knife . . . and a loaded pistol.

"It's all we have, but you need to be protected," she said, kissing my cheek. "If you don't need it, wonderful. Bring it back and we'll lock it away here. But the world is changing and we don't want you to wander into some war."

My parents nearly keeled over at the sight of their son, climbing out of this overloaded junker, carrying suitcases, blankets, a knife, and a gun.

"War?" I remember my father saying, incredulous. "Over what? The orange groves?"

Thankfully (and Thanksgiving had never taken such a personal turn), I never had to use any of my borrowed weapons and I handed them back, gently, upon my return to campus. The couple simply blushed, smiled, and shrugged. "You never know," was their reply. "It's always better to be safe than sorry." They had bought into the nationwide panic as Camelot neared its climax and a country's charm slowly soured. They had tried to talk me out of making the journey at all but, realizing I hadn't seen my family in several months, away from home for the very first time in my life, they gave in. But they made sure I could at least put up a fight, if it came to that.

I have lived that kind of charmed life. Someone has always been watching over the Giraffe.

It wasn't as if I had completely given up on the ministry. I still gave it token acknowledgment. I worked with children at an orphanage across the street from the college, teaching Sunday school and becoming a big brother to one of the youngsters whose father was a scout with the Dodgers and thus had little time for him. I attended chapel regularly, and when Carol and I began very preliminary marriage discussions, I quickly asked if she thought she could handle being a minister's wife. She had been the daughter of a Baptist church secretary for years, and so the church and its inner workings were no stranger to her. She said it would be no problem but, silently, she shuddered at the very thought.

I lost my academic scholarship, to the surprise of no one but my parents, and so returned home to Florida to try another tack. I had given my life great thought and decided that the ministry "just wasn't me." If I couldn't commit myself to being a decent student along that journey, what kind of pledge could I keep to God? Nobody was more upset about my leaving college than Carol, for it meant I was leaving her as well. And down deep, despite her struggles with the idea of being a preacher's wife, she knew she would handle it if that was what I wanted. But I knew it wasn't.

It was a terrible time for me. I felt that I was letting everyone down, from my own minister, who had taken me under his enormous wing, to my parents, who had seen my college grades and heard my stories and knew how poorly I was doing, to myself. It took me a long time before I could look myself in the mirror or offer more than a perfunctory prayer. I sat down with each of them—the minister, my parents, and myself—and had long, heartfelt talks. And though they all seemed to understand, I could see the disappointment in their eyes, read the heartbreak in their nods.

To this day, though my mother is a faithful viewer, always there, proudly proclaiming my merits to anyone who will listen ("I'm your best PR person," she never fails to say), she still harbors that ancient wish. And yet she knows where my talents lie.

"You always were a storyteller," she will say, a twinkle of sarcasm underlying her words. I've never known if that was good or bad and so, though she says it often, I leave it alone.

Good fortune has followed me throughout my chosen path, some opportunity always coming my way. I could have probably become manager of that Dairy Queen if I'd stuck with it instead of answering the ad in the paper.

I had accepted the assistant manager's job, in fact, to make ends meet while going on to the University of Florida, perhaps to study English or drama or missile crises. I had discovered a fond dislike for college, to be honest, and wasn't looking forward to a second chance, but I had been told that it was essential to any résumé. Moments after taking the DQ job, as I sat reading the morning paper, I noticed an advertisement that read simply, "Wanted: someone who can type and knows sports." I could do both and, curious, called the number. It was the local newspaper, and in a rash moment, I turned down the Dairy Queen and covered my first high school football game that very night. I was pretty awful, using every cliché imaginable, but sports editor Buddy Martin saw something he liked and I became his project.

He put me on a daily regimen, reading sports columns from around the country, changing them week after week. At night, he would sit at one end of the office and call me at the other, pretending to be a high school coach reporting his game statistics. I had to ask the right questions, break everything down, and have a short game story ready to hand him in fifteen minutes. Slowly, I began to learn my craft, develop a style, and love the business completely.

And one Friday evening, I had my first brush with death.

We would choose a local high school football game for me to cover each Friday night through the fall. Instead of sitting in the small, cramped press box, I preferred walking the sidelines, getting a real feel for the game and its emotions. One night, midway through the game in a small town a half hour away, the play came toward my side of the field. The running back was hit hard by several defenders and landed, twisted and unconscious, at my feet. The impact had knocked his helmet off and it rolled slowly away. I picked it up and saw the indentation, as though someone had taken a sledgehammer to it. They attended to the young man for what seemed like hours, very carefully took him from the field on a stretcher and, by ambulance, to a nearby hospital. In hours, he died of severe head trauma.

I wrote the story, as best I could, but found my mind and heart wandering back to that moment of impact, hearing the sound and feeling the terror. A young man's life was snuffed out, just as surely as if he had been crossing a street and been struck by a car. I was shaken for weeks afterward, trying to find the reasons in my religion for such a moment. I searched for answers but never found one.

A month or so later, I had just finished putting the afternoon paper to bed and was cleaning off my desk, getting ready to go to my afternoon classes at a local community college where I had enrolled for the fall, when the bells on the Associated Press wire machine began to ring urgently. It was just before noon on a Friday. The dateline was Dallas, Texas. Shots had rung out across a crowded parade route and President Kennedy had been hit. There were no further details to report at that moment.

Dazed, I drove the few miles to the campus and made my way to the English lit class. We were studying Dante's *Inferno,* discussing the devil's workshop, when my eyes drifted to the window and saw that they were lowering the flag on the tall pole outside. The professor noticed it too. Silently we closed our books and, without a word, made our way into the halls. John Kennedy had been our hero, all of us, and represented our best dreams. We were children, innocent and unknowing, willing to accept anyone in bright and shining armor as our idol then. All of that, every bit of it, died with the lowering of that flag to half-staff.

It rained hard that night and I was surprised that the football game to which I had been assigned was still scheduled. It was for the eight-man championship of Florida, a unique and wide-open brand of football developed almost exclusively for the smaller schools. But on this night, with the flags lowered and every eye full of tears, the game listless and unemotional, it became more of a symbol of how life must go on, regardless.

"It's what President Kennedy would've wanted," explained the principal of one of the tiniest high schools in all Florida, as though he and the president had talked about such an eventuality once upon a time.

Two days later, the commissioner of the National Football League, Pete Rozelle, said virtually the same words as he decided to allow his teams to play through the national tragedy. The man had touched us all, regardless of station.

I wandered from town to town, newspaper to newspaper, from Ocala to Tallahassee, to Melbourne and Lakeland, and finally to Miami, from *Ledger*s and *Democrat*s to *Star-Banner*s and *Herald*s, covering everything possible. I was learning much more than my craft along the way. We were a two-man staff in Tallahassee. The sports editor decided, in his infinite wisdom, that he would cover Florida State (which was plainly pitiful in those years) and I would cover Florida A&M (which wasn't). It had more to do with race than reality, for he simply did not want to cover the predominantly black university on the other side of town. I, on the other hand, was delighted to be covering anything and so I jumped into the role.

Nothing could have been better than being the only white person in either the stands or the press box, watching one of the great football programs in America, black or white, and reveling in the best halftime show, bar none, in the world. And when we would meet back at the office, post games, he would simply look down his nose at me as if to say, "Poor boy . . . but these are dues you're paying. Sooner or later, you'll cover the big time."

One Saturday night, after having enjoyed the remarkable Rattlers marching band and another A&M runaway victory that afternoon, I returned to lay out the Sunday morning paper. The boss was with the woeful Seminoles in Tuscaloosa playing Bear Bryant and Alabama's Crimson Tide. It had been a busy day and we only had so many column inches with which to work. I was tediously trying to figure out how to cram everything in, knowing I had to leave room for the boss's column down the entire left side of the front page. I cut and rewrote and fixed and left out some important news but had it down when he called from Alabama to dictate his column. Since I was the only one there, it was left to me to take it over the phone.

"Ugly game," I said.

"Ugly can't describe it."

"You ready to dictate?"

"Yeah, but it's gonna be a bit different," he said. "Ready?"

"Sure. Talk away."

"Okay, here we go. Dateline Tuscaloosa, Alabama. That's at the top, under my column head."

"Sure," I said, for that was always where it was.

"Now, go all the way to the bottom of the column. Leave everything else white. And put this: 'I sat here trying to figure out what to say about this horrendous game. And I thought and I thought and I thought . . .'"

"Wait. That's it?"

"Yeah. Clever, don'tcha think? It really is impossible to write about."

"Yes, but . . ."

"Just do it."

And so, the next morning, there was a column on the left side of the front sports page with nothing but a dateline at the top and one line at the bottom. He had wasted that many valuable column inches being cute. It was effective and had everyone laughing, but I had sacrificed solid news for all that white space. It was another lesson on my road. We are never larger than what we cover, and the space we are allowed, be it newsprint, radio, or television, must be considered as valuable as any mineral we mine. I could never have convinced him of that on that night or any other time, for he was far beyond that. But it allowed me another glimpse into the window of perspective.

chapter eight

from maravich to emmy

My final newspaper job, eight years after my debut, was with the *Atlanta Journal-Constitution* where I was offered the Atlanta Hawks NBA beat.

"Can you get along with egos?" my new boss asked me. "You'd better, 'cause the last guy couldn't, and that's why I had to move him off the Hawks."

"Never had any problem in the past," I answered.

"Yeah, but you never covered Pete Maravich in the past."

In my years in sports, I have worked with everyone from Muhammad Ali and Joe Namath to Michael Jordan and Tiger Woods. But never have I encountered such an enigma as Maravich. One of the greatest talents in basketball history, he absolutely lit up the court when he appeared; floppy socks down around his sneaker-tops, a mane of dark hair flying in the wind . . . he was a genius. And like many, he was as troubled as he was brilliant. When he decided he didn't like someone, he completely ignored the person—and that included everyone from teammates to reporters. He was a tough act, but one I thoroughly enjoyed being around. There was depth there, far beneath his basketball ability. When he became a born-again Christian in the years before his untimely death, those who knew only the legend were shocked. Those who bothered to spend any time with him understood and smiled knowingly.

"Whaddya think about God?" he asked me one quiet afternoon after practice. We were sitting alone in the stands and it became a moment in time I shall never forget.

"In what respect?"

"Oh, I dunno. I've been thinking about Him a lot lately."

"Any reason?"

"Probably not. But then again . . ." He looked at me and laughed. "Forget I brought it up. Bad for my image."

In a small office just off the main sports department those days, the wondrous Furman Bisher wrote his column every day, one of those who had been on my weekly reading regimen in the beginning as I was tediously learning my style. He would have been outraged at the misuse of column space that night in Tallahassee, for he fought for every word, every phrase, as though it were turf in a very private war. It was 1970, and he was thought to be on his way to retirement, nowhere near the raging bear that had once stalked this department, venting his wrath on whatever poor young soul got in his way. He had mellowed considerably by the time I arrived but still was a force. Thirty years later, he remained that way, turning out legendary lines at the age of eighty-two.

"That's Bisher's office over there," my new editor, a country boy named Lewis Grizzard, pointed out. "Used to be, he'd lock himself away in that room at eight in the morning, and when he came out at five or six, his fresh column finished, he looked like he'd been wrestling a bear. You could almost hear the struggle in there. We'd put our ears to the door and listen. But, boy, it was worth the fight, 'cause he could flat write."

Oddly enough, in those days, Grizzard could not . . . at least, not to our knowledge. He was our idea man, our layout man, a nuts-and-bolts editor who made sure the paper was laid out properly, had every story in its correct place, and got out on time. The homespun native Georgian left Atlanta for the *Chicago Sun-Times* a few years later, and when he returned, he was suddenly a writer. What had happened in the meantime, very few knew or understood. But here was this pencil pusher who was abruptly putting together wondrous pieces. He went on to become, to our utter amazement, a stand-up comic, a regular on the *Tonight Show*, an entertainer of sometimes crude but side-splitting style, who wrote book after book and had become a folk hero by the time of his early death. No one would have thought it when I sat across from him that hiring day.

"Want you to cover the Hawks," he drawled, tossing his cigarette on the hardwood floor and mashing it with a toe.

"Oh, and one more thing: my burning desire is to find out when the National Hockey League is coming to Atlanta. I know it is, I keep hearing the rumors, but nobody's been able to pin them down. I want you to break that story for me."

"Uh-huh, sure."

A year later, while covering the Hawks in New York, I slipped away to the NHL expansion meetings on Long Island and cornered some old friends. One whisper led to another, a nod and a dark-corner chat nailed down the word, and I had Grizzard's story. A team to be called the Flames would take the ice in Atlanta the following October, the first ice hockey ever played in the Deep South. And as a reward for that "scoop," I was given the hockey beat. Only problem was, I had never seen a game in my life. In fact, I was so poorly educated about the sport and its people that once, while in Miami, I was assigned to interview some NHL players who were there on vacation. I shuddered at the very thought of spending any time in the presence of such grizzled animals as I imagined these to be and found a way out of the assignment. Still, I had to face them sooner or later and had to learn their sport. I read voraciously that summer, watched films, studied, talked to players and coaches, writers and broadcasters, and spent a month in their first training camp in a tiny town between Montreal and Quebec City called Drummondville.

Summoning great courage, I made my way to the street corner outside our hotel that first night to greet the busload of players. I still was expecting toothless, scarred semi-literate goons, snarling and spitting and readying for their next brawl. To my everlasting surprise, the first player to step from the bus bringing them all in from Montreal was the veteran defenseman Pat Quinn, the toughest of them all. Legendary for his ice battles, he had made up for his lack of skating speed by becoming one of the league's bad guys. Surely the snarls would precede him down the bus steps. But dressed in tweed and turtleneck, smoking a pipe, he extended his hand, smiled, and won me over instantly. There followed a lovable cast of characters, the lot of whom I shall never, ever forget. For we all cast our fortunes together in those first memorable seasons.

When the regular season came, I sat extra close to the play-by-play announcer to learn the talk, the subtle nuances, the feel of the game as I had with football and basketball. It simply helped reinforce what I had just seen, hearing it put into the words of the knowing.

One night, I sat in with the legendary play-by-play announcer Jiggs McDonald on the broadcast to help out. His regular partner was sick. Just a few words here and there, certainly nothing either prophetic or wise, not from me. It turned from one game into several, and a few weeks later, the general manager of the radio station that carried the games asked if I'd ever considered broadcasting.

"What? And leave newspaper?" I was incredulous. And then he mentioned a salary figure. It's not like I could be bought or anything. I remember changing newspaper jobs in the early days for a five-dollar-a-week raise.

"We're offering you eighty-five dollars," responded the one-eyed man from Tallahassee, who could waste column space but not company money.

"Hey, we're rich. I was only making eighty dollars!"

After three years of doing the hockey games along with early-morning sportscasts and late night radio talk shows, a news director from an Atlanta television station called.

"You ever thought about doing TV?" Dick Williams asked.

It was becoming a joke how quickly my incredulity could be compromised by numbers. I had never contemplated television, had scorned the television sports anchors I had worked against over the years as being nothing more than pretty-boy readers, certainly never journalists. I was proud of my profession and had no desire to change. But thirty-five thousand dollars a year was a lot of money in those days. And so I began to learn a third side of the media business, another writing discipline.

In newspaper writing, I had had to develop a nose for column inches, making my contribution fit amidst the advertisements. Splitting my time in the field and on the desk made me appreciate the problems from both sides. As a writer you always want more space, but as an editor you take what you're given and try to find a way to make everything fit and everyone happy. It's never easy and that end of the business is forever thankless.

Writing for radio is theater of the mind. You must learn to paint mental pictures, take the listeners along on a magical ride. It is nothing but your word and their ears. Paint crisply, conservatively, judiciously, choosing your words like a brilliant oil; it can be the most satisfying of any medium. When you write for television, you must subjugate your ego for the sake of your story. Because it is obviously a visual performance, words can often become intrusive. They are necessary only to either underline the story, most times, or expand it. Nothing takes the place of good writing, be it on the printed page, radio, or television. But each has its own precise characteristics, and what I learned from the first, I adapted and modified to the second and took it to a different level with the third . . . all with the sometimes delicate and more often ham-fisted assistance of the editors.

Which of the three is the most satisfying? The one that ultimately touches the most people.

Seven years of weekends and weeknights after joining the television fray, I got the same call from CNN. My disbelief by then had disappeared for good.

"Wanna work for us?" asked Bill MacPhail that day at lunch.

"'Us' being Ted Turner?"

"Well, yes, in essence."

I had been in Atlanta at that point for fourteen years, had been around Turner much of that time, at his tiny Channel 17 studios, at the yacht yard as he was winning the America's Cup, at the baseball stadium once he'd purchased the Braves, or at courtside when he bought the Hawks. I liked the man. I thought he was brash and insensitive and very full of himself, but charm and charisma and dash overrode all of that. I had watched him don a Santa Claus costume and beard and beg his audience at Christmas for cash donations to help him keep his small, struggling station on the air. And what seemed like a century later, I watched him donate a billion dollars of his own money to the United Nations. The road in between was marked with raw, absolute, often frustrating genius. Still, I doubted I could work for him.

"You probably won't see him much at all," said MacPhail. "And he is strictly hands-off in our department. Never interferes. He's been a great boss so far."

And so, in 1984, I became a Turner man and likely will always be, though *always* and *never* have been poor choices of words for me, ultimately.

"Thought you said you'd never, ever, ever work for that guy," my father said with a laugh when I told him the news. "Thought . . ."

"Dad," I said, "don't you know me any better than that by now?"

Over the decades, I had been a beat man covering Little League, high school and college teams, pro football, the NBA, the NHL, golf, tennis, swimming, soccer, racing, archery, bowling . . . nearly every sport played by man, woman, or animal. I traveled with the Miami Dolphins of the NFL, the Atlanta Hawks of the NBA, and the Atlanta Flames of the NHL over the seasons, living in their training camps, becoming a part of their entourages, learning not only their businesses but also their lives.

My father lived vicariously, taking great secondhand joy in my stories and travels. Though they lived in the town where I began my newspaper career and never once lived where they could see me or read my work on a regular basis until I went to CNN, he kept close track. If I didn't send him a clipping or videotape, I'd rehash the story long-distance.

"How many people got mad at you today?" He'd laugh through the phone midway through our weekly call. "You still being bad?"

It was a moment when I was good, however, that he took to his grave, savoring the telling and retelling like a friendly old sweater.

"Tell 'em again," he would urge me as he lay dying, "about Broadway."

The Manhattan banquet hall was packed with friends and associates the night I won my first national Emmy in the spring of 1998. I should have asked Dick Enberg, with whom I shared the honor, how one handles such a moment, for this was surely his twentieth, just something else to collect dust in a corner of his office. Instead, I simply wandered in semicircles, calling everyone I knew, wiping the tears away, the post-ceremony party babbling madly around me. To most in the room, this meant very little, another night on the town, another victory, another loss, "I'm honored just to be nominated," "I'd like to thank my parents." But to me, it seemed so much larger than any of that, the first Emmy ever won by a sportscaster from our network. Validation. Awards, for some reason, had always been important to me . . . until I won my first local Emmy.

I had been in television only a year but had always heard about the Emmys, how important they were, how prestigious. I assumed that if you won one, your life would instantly change. Raises would be thrown your way and job offers would come from far and near. And then I won one. I strutted into the office the following Monday, ready for the ticker tape, only to find it was simply another day.

"What're you gonna do for me today?" was the prevalent response.

"You're never as good as winning an award and never as bad as losing one," was the way one wise boss always put it.

But this was my first national Emmy. This put me on a plane with the big network boys. I had been nominated five times previously and the losing made that wise boss's theory lack a bit of reality. I wanted that trophy and everything it supposedly represented.

I looked for someone who would appreciate that, who would understand, but the faces that night began to blur and so I clutched my golden statue under my tuxedoed arm and proceeded to make my way the ten blocks back to my hotel. Just me, my Emmy, and a huge smile, making our way down Broadway. If it had been raining,

I would have been Gene Kelly, kick-splashing my way home. Not a soul seemed to notice, being New York City, except for one homeless man.

"Whatcha got there?" he muttered from the shadows.

"Emmy."

"Never heard of her. You do look shiny, though. Got a buck?"

I gave him two.

It was a moment in my life that will live, bright and fresh with lush background music, forever. That it made little difference to my career was beside the point.

It was a mental picture that never failed to break a huge grin across my father's face.

"Oh, that's such a great story." He would laugh. "I can see you now."

It didn't seem to matter to him that his son had lost his calling. He had found his love.

chapter nine

the marriage test

Though I never looked back after spurning the pulpit, knowing I was not of that cloth, I also felt myself slowly sliding away from the church itself. Work often took me away on Sundays, to games and the like. And without a mother knocking down my bedroom door, it became easy to sleep in. Disillusionment reared its ugly head as well, separating me farther. Though there probably was no precise moment when the door opened and I walked out, there was a defining circumstance that made me turn and look at all that I had grown up with, all that I had believed, and wonder.

After a period of indecision and separation, Carol and I decided it was time to marry, so we went to my minister, the one who had been my tour guide through the mountain range of youthful emotions. He had been my inspiration and, though he saw me lose my calling, had never given up on me.

Until the moment that we came to ask him to marry us.

"I will," he said with a giant smile. "I'd be delighted. But I'd like you both to take a little test to see if you're truly suited for one another."

We looked at one another in astonishment. What was he talking about? Aren't we the best judges of something so personal and serious? What could a test prove? And what if his little test decided we weren't a match? Would he refuse? Could he?

"No," I said meekly, "I don't see why we have to do that. And I don't think we will."

"Then," he quietly returned, "I cannot, in good faith, marry you."

This was my pastor, the man I so totally believed in. We had gone on trips together, held hands and prayed together, been part of a great (and now disintegrating) dream together. And now he was rejecting us. He had undergone radical changes over those last few years, taken seminars and courses that had shed new light on the workings of his profession. I remember the Sunday morning sermons after he had been off somewhere getting illuminated were often excruciatingly long and labored as if we, his congregation, had become his students. I was a great fan of the fire-and-brimstone style of preaching. I could listen to a man with a Bible in one hand and a lightning bolt in the other for hours, enraptured by his enthusiasm and spirit. But when he began lecturing, I knew we were in for a long Sunday.

And now he was rejecting us.

Ironically, the gentle pastor of the church we had attended as a family in Edinboro, Pennsylvania, had retired to a wonderful little house of worship in the middle of an orange grove just a half hour or so from where we lived in Florida. And so, with hat in hand, I called and asked if he would see Carol and me. I had been one of his "children" whom he would call to the altar every Sunday morning during services. If I had remained on course, I would have chosen him as my role model. Good and kind, everything I always thought a minister should be. He and his first wife had been missionaries during World War II and were prisoners of war in the Philippines. They had a small child and Ruth gave him the meager ration of food she received, thus starving herself. She was never healthy again and eventually died after they had moved south. But he always took care of her, remained attentive and devoted, and to be honest, I didn't know why we hadn't called him first.

"Of course I will marry you," he said quickly, as though flabbergasted there would be any question. When I told him of the test, he simply shook his head and said, "I'll marry you two, no tests needed."

And he did. But while that should have renovated my attachment to the Spirit, it lay instead in tatters. And I still, decades later, work at retrieval. Would it take my own father's death to bring me back? And where would I be, once (and if) I got back?

I learned, through my father's final months, that my God and I have a relationship, private and pure. I know that He hears me, know that He watches over me and has kept me all these years. I thank Him often and try to give back in other, subtle ways. But He became much more real, much more important to me, much more of a steadying influence, in the days of my father's death.

Dad slept much of the day through the last months. First, he rested in his living room chair, the television only background noise. When he was finally bedfast, the sleep was nearly constant, and he woke only to eat a meager meal or pass on his latest dream-adventure. My mother's sorrow became tainted with loneliness. They had been partners more than half a century, rarely out of each other's sight. When she went to the store, so did he, joined at the heart forever. She could count on one hand the number of times they had slept apart, after the war, and now she might as well have been alone. Because he needed elevation while he slept, doctors recommended he get a hospital bed.

And so in the final few months, though they were still in the same room each night, still able to hold hands as they always had, saying their prayers together, there was that tiny separation, two single beds pushed together. It seemed minimal to us and yet to them it was a chasm far wider than ever before in their marriage. Another subtle indication of what was to come.

As time—and Dad's life—passed, I found myself hurting deeper than I ever expected. I would be sitting on the deck, painting in my studio upstairs, or writing in my office downstairs when suddenly I would simply break down uncontrollably, weeping like a child. Through the tears, which were rather frightening to me, I forced myself to look at the larger picture. Why was this affecting me this way?

And I would have this conversation with myself, often:

Why the tears?

He is my father.

Yes, but all fathers die. This one a bit early, perhaps, but not far outside the modern range.

But I feel that I'm just getting to know him.

You've had a good couple of decades as friends. Lotsa guys don't get anywhere near that much.

I just learned how to tell him I love him. I wasted all that time.

Yes, but at least you did tell him. There's something to be said for that.

I'm losing a friend.

And?

I'm staring at myself lying there.

Finally, the bottom line.

Look at him. I look just like him, twenty-three years younger, that's all.

You're worried about the baldness thing.

72

I never thought I looked that much like him until a couple of weeks ago, a new nurse came in and I started to introduce myself to her. "Oh, no, you don't need to tell me who you are. You are your father's son."

Aren't we all?

But I always looked like Mom: light, fair-skinned. Chuck always looked like Dad: dark hair, olive skin. Though Dad was Swiss, he often passed for a dozen different nationalities—Hawaiian, Jewish, Italian—nobody could peg him as Swiss. We would go out as a family and nobody could accuse my brother and me of being adopted. And now here I am, crossing boundaries.

So?

So I'm looking at my own mortality.

chapter ten

the dreams of a dying man

Everywhere I turned, I looked for solace, for answers, comparative shopping. Very few folks I met had ever encountered liver disease quite like his and so they would shrug their shoulders and fold their answers in mock prayer.

It was much easier with the prostate cancer. Perhaps the fact that neither Mom nor Dad ever seemed to know it wasn't *prostrate* helped make it seem less deadly.

"That's the horizontal disease, right?" we'd ask so seriously. "You get that lying down, right?"

And they would simply talk on.

"Tough getting cancer of the prostrate," we'd quip, chuckling among ourselves later. "Maybe if he stood up, it'd go away."

Although we were fully aware of the deadly consequences, the simple levity of the innocent malaprop helped lessen the fear. Whistling past the cemetery.

"We're awful."

"Yeah, awful. But you don't suppose . . . ?"

"Nah, he'll be fine. I just have this feeling he will be."

As he waged his radiated war against the cancer just a year before the liver began to spill, he called with almost daily numbers, seeming to delight in the entire process. If he was worried, he never let on. It seemed a scientific venture to him, the radiation aimed a certain way for a certain amount of time, to attack the cancer just a certain way. He would have hated the agony of chemotherapy but seemed absorbed by this painless intrusion into his gut.

It was a war he could tell he was winning, simply by the PSA numbers, and they lifted him by the week. After failing so often at so many ventures over his lifetime, he was actually going to win one now.

In the midst of his skirmish, I had a chance to spend a day in Florida with the legendary golfer Arnold Palmer, who had, just that morning, been given a clean bill of health after his own very public battle with prostate cancer.

"Tell your dad he can lick it," Palmer told me. "What are his PSA numbers?" I told him, and he responded, "That's good. They're going down. Soon, they'll probably stabilize and he'll be as good as new. You see, what'd I tell you? Catch this stuff early and it's beatable. You give him my best, and tell him I'm praying for him."

I did that, on the phone that very night, and I could almost see my father light up through the line.

"Arnold Palmer said that?" he whispered. "You talked to him about me?"

"Sure. You guys are in this thing together. He says you're gonna be fine."

And he was, for a few months.

■ SEPTEMBER 1999

"Who are those people outside the door?" he asked one afternoon.

"People?"

"Well, I guess I was dreaming," he said, and it was becoming hard to distinguish between the parallel universes as the liver disintegrated, "but I saw shadows walking back and forth outside the room."

"Shadows? People?"

"Yes, but I couldn't recognize anybody. They were just people, dressed in black. Except one."

"And . . . ?"

"Yeah, one was all in white, just sorta mixed in among the ones in black."

I was told this was a "very normal" dream. I hated that. I wanted all of his reveries to be astonishingly unique, unlike any others ever recorded. They were fascinating to me, a world I had never experienced before. Though I lived in my own nightly dream world, a light sleeper with a constant finger on my subconscious, I never was able to make much sense of mine. But his on the other hand, as he slowly died, seemed prophetic, each word, each scene seeming to paint the mural of his demise.

When I heard of this one, I pressed him about it.

"So," I said, sitting at the side of his bed, "the shadows . . . you never saw a face?"

"No, never a face."

"Were they always outside the room?"

"No. I woke up one night and the one in white was all alone, standing by my bed. Over there, by the closet."

"Did he say anything? Was it a he?"

"I guess it was a he, I dunno. And no, he didn't say a thing. Just stood there."

"Did you recognize him?"

"No, I don't think so. He didn't have a face."

Soon, the Hospice workers said, having dealt on a daily basis with this, faces would appear. Just wait. He will see faces. It's very normal. And when he does, it will signal the end. I don't know how anyone knows that for a fact but it's an eerie fable spread freely.

I awoke one night during all of this in a numbing panic. Suddenly, one of my own dreams had become stunningly real. I had been standing in my parents' tiny kitchen when Dad walked out of the bedroom and came to my side. He was younger and bathed in white, almost glowing. He put his hands on my shoulders and smiled at me.

"Go home," he said to me in my dream, "go home and don't come back just for me."

And then he hugged me.

The dream had come days before my last visit, long before he told me of his own vision. Was there a connection between his "white shadow" and mine? And the figure in white who stood next to his bed; was he seeing an image of himself? Was this a variation on the white light in the corner of the operating room—the window to heaven—we have heard of for years? Would an eventual face bring the final dream?

Normal.

chapter eleven

heavenly requests

Dad worried in his later years, as almost everyone does these days, about developing Alzheimer's, the insidious disease that burrows into the brain and scrambles all the wiring into chaos.

"Don't worry, pal," I teased him, "you'll never know you have it. It's us who have to worry."

Whistling past another graveyard.

I had played golf occasionally with an older man burdened with the early stages of the illness. He would hit his drive and wander aimlessly down the fairway, not knowing what he was looking for. We would have to lead him to the ball and tell him it was his turn to hit. At that point, most times, he would click back in and carry on. But it wouldn't last very long and made for frustrating after-noons, both for him and for his partners. In the end, he would sim-ply ride along with the rest of us, enjoying the day, rarely recognizing us or the game we were playing.

In the midst of this and my father's own concerns, I flew one day to Upstate New York to tape another *Sporting Life* segment that would hit home in more ways than I could count.

Ted Darling was the voice of the Buffalo Sabres. From the very inception of that National Hockey League franchise, he had painted word pictures to an adoring radio audience, and few announcers were better in that very difficult business. We would get together whenever I was in town on assignment for a quick chat or a bite to eat. In the early '90s I heard rumors. He liked his drink and those he worked with slowly began to suspect he was nipping on the job, something that would have been absolutely abhorrent to him in better days. But suddenly he would almost mentally disappear for a second during a broadcast—forgetting a Sabre's name, having problems remembering the score—little things he had never, ever done before. They were about to fire him but, thankfully, ordered a physical checkup first.

When I showed up at the front door with a camera crew that crisp winter morning in 1997, he stared straight through me.

"Come in, Jim," his wonderful wife, Sheila, said, forcing a smile on a weary face. "He may recognize you, but maybe not."

He was just fifty-three, but while his eyes still sparkled, there was a vacancy that frightened us all. He smiled but didn't know why. Grandchildren crawled into his lap and loved him but he wasn't there anymore. We went for a walk around the block, a forced reunion, but it was as though we were total strangers. I tried to talk hockey. He simply nodded. I knew Ted had been so proud of his son Joel, who was a producer with the Canadian Broadcasting Company in Toronto, and I brought up his name, but nothing clicked. There were moments, flashes, when I thought he knew me, but they disappeared quickly and we settled back into a strange stroll.

He had early Alzheimer's disease and would be dead less than a year after I did his story. From being at the point of firing the man to quickly saluting him, the Sabres took my story and played it on the arena's big screen during intermission of one game as a tribute. Fans stood in silent, tearful honor.

Another headstone added to my show's cemetery.

I thought of Ted Darling often during my sessions with Dad, so grateful for the clarity. When Dad was able to stay awake for hours at a time, alert and yet knowing that his days were dwindling, we talked of death and what it was like. The father sitting in his chair, the son next to him on a stool, a hand resting gently on an arm, an interview in process. We had never been a family of touch. Hugging had only become "legal" in recent years, kissing never accepted between men. But as he prepared to take his leave, that all changed. I wanted to touch him as often as possible, to smooth his white hair and hold his hand. They'll probably say that's quite normal, too, but it hadn't been for us.

"Everything is shutting down inside," he said, very understandable, his teeth still in at that point. "It's happening so fast. The liver isn't working much anymore and so that's putting a lotta pressure on the other organs to handle things. My insides are closing up shop. I can feel it."

I tried to imagine.

"Are you scared?"

"Kinda . . . but I'm also looking forward to it. I know what's ahead. I'm sure. I know I'll get to see my mom and dad again, my grandparents and theirs. I can't wait to tell my grandfather all about the expressway system. He loved to drive and I always thought he'd be amazed at the way the highways are now. But then again, he probably already knows, huh?"

It was a message he had been planning on delivering for years. Every time I would drive him into the city in the years before his illness, the lanes of the superhighway spreading out on either side, he would shake his head and say the same words: "My granddad would be amazed at this." He would say it every single trip. "He loved to drive, but this would have frightened him, I think."

Now he was on his way to finding out.

Dad's brother came to see him and they sat together in the bedroom for two hours, settling things forever. Jack and Dad had gone their separate ways, as brothers sometimes do, and though they had occasionally visited, there had never seemed to be much warmth and they drifted apart. The phone calls were seldom, the letters almost nonexistent . . . Christmas cards, little else. Though Dad and Jack had been close as children, and though they had both looked lovingly after their little sister, Betty, the miles that separated them all in adulthood were a heavy, seemingly impenetrable barrier. And when Dad's parents had to be moved into a nursing home, the rift seemed to grow even wider. Dad's father, the old Swiss machinist, had settled into dementia before death, sadly wandering the streets first and then the halls of the home, never knowing who or where or when or why anymore. And my grandmother had lingered, unhappily, for years before joining him.

She died, as she had wanted to for so long, at the large old Lutheran rest home just north of Pittsburgh. My parents lived at that time in the mountains of North Carolina, a forced retirement after so many years with the U.S. Postal Service in Florida. Carol and I were on a short vacation in the panhandle of Florida, and when the phone call came, we were consumed by the breaking news of a large commercial airliner crash in Dallas. So wrapped up in it, in fact, that we nearly didn't answer the phone in the small beachfront condo. Hundreds were dead, some from Atlanta. Would we know any one of them? But a ringing phone at a vacation stop could mean only one of two things—a sales pitch from the front office or bad news. With that in mind, I remember hesitating and then answering.

"Grandma Huber has died," came my mother's first words.

Though it was expected, it still came as jarring news. She was ninety-six and went peacefully, so they said.

"Can I talk to Dad?" I asked my mother.

His familiar melodic voice, saddened a pitch, came in a few seconds. "Are you okay?"

"Oh, yeah," he said matter-of-factly. "She had been ready for a long time, you know."

"Yes, I do. When are y'all going up for the funeral?"

There was an uncomfortable pause.

"I don't know; I don't think we're going," he said.

"What? Not go? How could you not go to your own mother's funeral?" And then I caught myself, ashamed, for I knew a bit about their financial situation. "Dad, I'll tell you what. What if we send you the plane tickets? Whaddya say?"

"I dunno. Let me talk to your mother and we'll call you back. That's awful nice of you. I just don't know."

Within the hour, he called me back. "I appreciate the offer," he said, "but your mother can't go and I don't wanna go alone. It just wouldn't be right. Your mother's legs are so bad right now she can't go, and I won't go without her. I can honor Mom just as easily here as there. She's not there anymore, y'know."

"If that's what you want. But if you change your mind," I said, "just call. If you need anything at all . . ."

But he didn't change his mind, and though that stayed with my father the rest of his life, a burden he couldn't share, it likely fueled the family fire. His brother and sister and their families didn't have near the financial problems that Dad and Mom had and surely had a tough time understanding his decision. There was a gaping hole in that funeral line and it likely hurt them as much as it did Dad.

But Jack and his wife had lost a daughter, Jackie, years before to heart disease when she was just eight. And when the doors to heaven are apparently about to open, there are messages to pass along. So they settled whatever had stood between them that day behind closed doors, and as Jack was leaving, he reminded Dad to make sure and look her up.

My father, over time, took many such requests.

And he fully intended to revisit us all. He had definite ideas about what his role would be in the hereafter.

"Oh, you'll know when I come to visit," he would say, laughing with my brother and his wife. "I'll just rattle the chandelier a little. Just to say hello."

He had nothing specific for me. He said he'd just surprise me. Right. "Oh, look, the lights are flickering; it's Grandpa! Say hello, kids."

"Who is that man dressed in gray?" he asked one day, as time grew nigh. "And whose baby is he holding?"

There was no one in the bedroom except the two of us.

"What's he look like, Dad?"

"Kinda rough. Nothing more. I don't recognize him."

I asked him the next day if he had seen the man in gray again. He said every time he saw him after that, nobody was around to tell. When we were, the man was gone.

His eyes, though shut, were restless, jumpy. You could almost see the dreams from the outside. I would sit and watch him, comfortable simply being close.

Suddenly his eyes opened.

"Where were you?" I asked.

"In a bar during the war," said the man who wouldn't know the inside of a bar if you took him there. "There were English and American sailors drinking together."

He was navy, South Pacific, World War II, a time he never talked about. Something serious happened there but he wouldn't discuss it with us . . . ever. We would ask, often, but he would simply shake it off. It took him years to accept one of us buying a Japanese car or television set. He seemed stunned that I had enjoyed myself, had thoroughly loved the people, during my work at the 1998 Winter Olympics in Nagano. I tried to tell him how warm and courteous, how completely devoid of guile, they were to me. I tried to tell him of the one night in particular that I shall remember forever.

I was walking back to the hotel from the International Broadcast Center, I told him. It was late and the snow was falling softly, making the lights along the six-mile trip through the town dance in glory. Time meant nothing as I strolled, looking into the darkened shop windows, listening to the pleasant whispers of music, thoroughly entranced by a magical land. I came to one small store of knickknacks and antiques, and noticed a light coming from the back room. I cupped my hands along the front window, looked closer, and saw an older woman kneeling on the floor, painting something.

I tapped cautiously on the window. She turned and saw me. I was afraid she would hide or turn off the lights or call the police but she simply knelt there, looking back at me. I motioned for her to hold up what she was painting so I could see. She smiled, slowly got to her feet and shuffled to the door, unlocked it, and bowed. Come in, she motioned. It was nearly eleven o'clock on a cold, snowy night and I was obviously a foreigner. And yet she had not the slightest apprehension about letting me in. Perhaps it was the huge Olympics credential still hanging around my neck. We were honored guests in their land and everyone I met went out of his way to make us welcome. She ushered me to the back room and pointed to a cushion on the floor.

"Sit," she said. It may have been one of the few English words she knew, for the rest of our time together was spent in search of a common communication. She brought out hot tea and some cookies and made me eat and drink, then showed me, lovingly, the lamp shades she had been painting. They were delicate and beautiful works of art. We laughed as we struggled to make ourselves understood. She kept two Japanese-to-English dictionaries on a counter and made good use of them that night. Finally, feeling guilty that I had kept this ancient woman up so late, I rose to say good night. She smiled beautifully, bowed, and put up her palm. "Wait."

She was gone for just a few moments, returning with a small doll that she handed to me. I had been in Japan long enough to know to never protest such an offering and so I took the gift, bowed in return, and thanked her profusely, wishing I had something in return. All I had was my biggest smile and it seemed to be enough.

"Arigato gozimas," I stumbled and she blushed at my attempt. As I finished my walk that night, I thought over and over again of such a life as this. Of how blessed I was to have had such a moment. And it would be neither the first nor the last there.

I told my father all of this, of the culture and the spirit and the wonderful peace of the Japanese people, but he simply said something about it "looking pretty there on TV," and let it go at that. I wrote an Internet column about my experiences there, for I was certain mine wasn't the only father still fighting the war within himself. The words likely fell on deaf eyes.

Once while we were dining in an Atlanta restaurant, a Japanese television crew doing a documentary on life in the American South came through and stopped at our table. As the reporter asked me questions in his halting English, Dad turned very pale, went into a shell for the rest of the evening, and refused to talk about it.

"What's wrong with you, Dad?"

"Nothin'."

"It's okay," my mother said. "Let him be. He's fine, probably just tired."

He had been an underwater welder working off a repair ship called the *Hector*. It's doubtful that he saw much more than peripheral action, but such a bloody, confusing exercise can have long-lasting, devastating effects. He chose to keep them locked deep within. There was a chance of finally breaking through that barrier and, ironically, it came during his last spring on earth. We had gone on the Internet, such a vast and exciting place to him, and found that there was going to be a reunion of his shipmates in San Diego. The *Hector* had been scuttled after the war, turned into scrap, but it was still as real as if it were docked at Pearl Harbor once more. We talked about it, started to make plans for it. I made contact with a few of his mates by E-mail and they remembered him well. But on the weekend of this visit in the spring of 1999, as I sat at the computer planning his reunion, he excused himself. We were alone in the house.

When he came back, he looked weak.

"Are you okay?"

"I dunno. I'm bleeding again."

"How long has this been going on?" I asked.

"Just a few weeks. I dunno what it is. Doesn't hurt or anything but it's kinda scary."

"You seen a doctor about it?"

"Yeah, but they don't know what's causing it. Could be anything. I'm okay, just getting old."

"Better than the alternatives."

That reunion came and went as he was battling for survival that furious June. If they had planned to go, there wouldn't have been room on that calendar.

Perhaps the dream replaced it.

"The Americans in the bar were talking the English guys into getting a U.S. flag tattooed on their backs," he continued remembering.

"What about you?"

"Oh, I was just watching."

"How come you never got a tattoo, Dad? You know, maybe with Mom's name on your arm or something?"

"What if we'd broken up?"

He laughed at the very idea of it. He was hours from death, the doctors predicted, and yet the toothless laughter came easily.

chapter twelve

last chance to say good-bye

Over the months after we were told Dad had little time left, I visited as often as possible. Sometimes stopping off on a business trip, simply for a couple of hours, sometimes for a day or two, but whatever time we shared was good. I told myself constantly that if *this* was the last time I would see him, I'd make it the best. And so we would talk, more than we ever did before, frank and honest. He loved hearing about my travels, about the latest stories. He became as involved in them as I did.

And I said my good-byes. Dozens of them.

"I love you, Dad."

It was the first time in my life I'd ever told him that eye to eye, and it felt awkward and planned, as it did when he said it back to me. We had mumbled it at the end of phone calls for the last few years.

"Um, love you, Dad."

"Me too."

Though we were never close as father and child, we slowly grew into a wonderful adult relationship, working on home projects, him trying to teach me all about wiring and sawing and nailing, and me not learning, just enjoying the time together. But I never told him to his face I loved him until he was dying. It seemed important that he know, as much to me as to him.

Why is that so difficult for fathers and sons, for men, in general? I had told my mother for years, for decades, that I loved her, but I had to practically force the words out of my mouth as my father and I grew closer.

"I love you" became easy compared with "good-bye." I wondered just how many ways I could say it and how often, for each time we parted over the fifteen months on death watch could have been the last. It became a mental game. This time will be the best, the most eloquent. Maybe I can clear the room this time, just me and him. Maybe I can ask Mom to join me. Do I try it standing? Should I just write something to him? A chicken way out, but I seem to be much better with words on paper than ad-libbed.

It was difficult, and yet better each time.

The last time—and I knew (pretty sure, maybe positively) this was the last time—I simply leaned over his cool face, kissed his brow, and whispered how much I loved him, how special he was, and then turned and walked out quickly so he would not see me break down. The hoax that had visited him that very afternoon surely would be avenged soon. Another dream, edging upon a nightmare.

"I was at the gates of heaven," he said hesitantly, as if he didn't really want to remember this one. "A man had a sheet of paper and asked my name and I told him. He looked and said, 'Yes, you're here, come on in.'

"When I got inside, there was a huge room with barriers and road cones. We were asked to walk around those and there were people checking us. A maze, kinda. It was sorta like boot camp, honestly. And then we had to hurry up a stairway with a guy timing us."

"You were walking on your own? No walker, no wheelchair, no problems?"

"Yeah, on my own. Anyway, I got to the top of the stairs and they ushered me into this enormous room and there, on a big throne, sat the tallest man I've ever seen. About eight feet tall with a big bushy beard. And he said, 'All of you, put all your money in this box over here.'

"And I said, 'Oh, no, you don't! This is a hoax!' And I ran down the stairs, them chasing me. I ran out the door and there was a pickup truck waiting. I asked the driver for a ride and he said, 'Hop in the back.' And we sped off."

He looked up at me, deep furrows creasing his forehead. He was angry. He wanted heaven so badly but this had been a cheap imitation. Scam artists at the Pearly Gates? The worst kind of purgatory?

"Oh," he groaned, "I'm so tired."

He was never a literate man, despite being a voracious reader. His grammar was sporadic and yet his mind worked like a great sponge, absorbing everything he came in contact with. We traded books over the years on every conceivable subject, and while Mom sat knitting, he would dive into yet another adventure. A part of his dream world, of course, his way of escaping.

In his later years, he even tried his hand at writing a children's book about the Cherokee Indians and a magic mineral found in the mountains of North Carolina. In retirement, he and my mother had worked to stay busy at a gemstone site near Asheville. Dad gave tours. Always the storyteller, with a dream thrown in for good measure, he was in his element and the book, titled *The Adventures of Little Drum,* sprang from his days there. Perhaps an omen too.

They walked back to their village slowly, deep in their own thoughts.

One woman had lost a son moments earlier, another her sister. Death was a part of their daily routine, it seemed, as they struggled for survival in the mountains of the Great Carolina. What the Great Father didn't take, the mountains did. Still, it was not easy to either understand or accept. And so they quietly went, one by one, to their individual wigwams to be alone with their emotions.

A tear stained the white chalk that powdered Little Deer's face during her work in the cave. She knelt before the fire, alone now, busily preparing her family's meal. One by one, the tears came, sizzling into the fire.

"What is it, Little Deer?"

Black Hawk dropped the large turkey he had just killed and ran to his mate's side. She seldom cried, seldom showed emotion.

"The cave fell," she quietly explained. "Three were crushed. Two more are missing."

How odd, Black Hawk thought. The men are called braves as we hunt our meals and fight our enemies. And the women and children of this tribe? All they do is face the cave, day in and day out, digging for the soft white stone. Bravely, for the danger is far greater there than in the forest.

"You rest," he told his wife, "I will get some braves and see if we can dig the last two out."

The Spiritual Leader's haunting chant could be heard throughout the mountainside as he welcomed the dead to their final resting place. As he reached each body, he would stop chanting and—with grand eloquence—place a sheet of mica over each body.

How strange, that the same cave which had taken these lives would contribute burial protection. The mica was mined by the Wolf tribe in large blocks, from which dozens of sheets of mineral could be peeled. It was thought to contain magic powers and so, when placed on the body, was not only considered grand decoration in life but the perfect guide to the Great Beyond in death.

He would send each chapter along to me for editing and I passed the finished product to friends in the industry, hoping for a favor. None ever came. He had it copyrighted by the Library of Congress in 1994 and both longhand and typewritten versions rest in a box still somewhere. Was it good? It was his and I still regret its lying in waste because he had dreamed great and glorious dreams of one final moment of success while writing it. Of finally getting something right. Of finding a bit of a career after a lifetime of jobs. I kept at it, telling him that one more publisher was going to take a look at it. But he knew. And the dreams were dashed at its rejection.

There was a great garden in that mind of his, fertile and ready for any kind of dream to crop up. And as he lay there, asleep twenty hours a day, the harvest was substantial. If we do remember just a small percentage of our dreams, I can only imagine what he was never able to bring to the surface in those final days.

He was a great paradox. Though his grammar was poor, his writing was delicate and precise. Though raised an introvert, he grew to be the life of any gathering. Though a mysterious ailment that seemed to run in his family made the shaking in his hands worse and worse through the years, making it nearly impossible for him to sip coffee without messy spills, he was an intricate craftsman, able to whittle the minutest detail and weave with great dexterity. Among his favorite things to make were dream catchers, the colorful Native American designs that hang in a bedroom to snare dreams.

One afternoon, near the end, his three great-granddaughters who lived nearby were at the mall with their mother when they spotted a strange new thing.

"What's that, Mama?"

"I think it's called a dream catcher," she answered. "Papa used to make those."

"Do they work?"

"He sure believed they did."

"Can we buy it for Papa? Can we? Can we? Maybe it will catch all his bad dreams before they get to him."

They pooled their pennies and, with some help from their mother, bought the dream catcher with its brown and white feathers, took it to his bedside, and proudly placed it on the dresser. They put it close to his left ear, for that's where they figured the dreams surely entered.

He never saw it, as far as we know, for he never truly awakened alert after that. But that dream catcher remained there, on guard, and when his ashes were entombed in a columbarium near where they lived, it joined him there. Catching dreams for an eternity.

chapter thirteen

the silver lining

■ AUGUST 1994

As I wandered among the incredible gathering of humanity that made up *The Sporting Life*—the sick and the disabled, the grieving and the gifted—I found a few people so overwhelming in their depth and purity that I knew I had been in the presence of someone very special. But rarely someone with the aura of an angel.

Andrea Jaeger could have lost her childhood as so many other teenage athletes have, could have kept those long pigtails and traded on her tennis stardom forever. But as she was touring the tennis world, she would often disappear for hours at a time, only to be found in the children's ward of some local hospital, playing games, telling stories, laughing, being a kid. As she watched children suffer and die, something struck her deep inside and she knew what her life's work must be.

An injury forced her to retire from tennis early and she wound up in Aspen, Colorado, where she and some friends began to build a dream. They would somehow bring children with life-threatening illnesses to this beautiful landscape for a few days at a time, to brighten what were surely dark times. And one day, maybe build a ranch where they could all stay. It seemed like such a pipe dream in its infancy, but when the first handful of children arrived—hobbling, bandaged, eaten by cancer—and she saw their smiles, a furious fire was stoked.

"It was so hard, so emotional, and yet so rewarding," she told me on our first of several visits to document her story. "Some of these kids had never seen a mountain, never been on a horse, never fished or ridden in a canoe or eaten hot dogs out under the stars. Sure, we've lost some of them and I still get all teary when I'm saying good-bye at the airport because I don't know if I'll ever see them again. But just to have given them some laughter for a little while, well, it's worth the tears."

As hard as she dreamed, she worked even harder, almost desperately raising funds across America for the Kids Stuff Foundation. An elderly couple donated a piece of land worth $10 million inside the Aspen city limits where she would finally build the place she called the Silver Lining Ranch. Finally, in the summer of 1999, nearly a decade after she began her quest, she opened its doors for the first time to an awestruck collection of twenty youngsters from across the country, all of them fighting for their lives. They would spend a week there, one of seven such sessions planned throughout the year.

An artist had come and spent eight months turning each bedroom into its own special creation, a tiny imaginary world where these young people could lie on their backs, look around them, and forget for a moment or two what was going on inside them. One room was a land of castles and unicorns, another was the sky with planets and stars and streaking spaceships, yet another was a jungle. From ceiling to floor, each room became an enchanted land. There were a full medical facility downstairs, a playroom with every gadget imaginable, a restaurant-sized kitchen, and a view to die for. The majestic mountains beckoned each child to climb higher.

"This is yours," she proudly announced to them, sweeping the arm that once dazzled opponents when it held a tennis racket. The majority of these children had never heard of Andrea Jaeger, didn't know stories of her athletic prowess long before they were born. All they knew of her was this strange and beautiful gift she was giving them.

"This is your silver lining."

And she was their angel.

I stood off to the side that day and thought of a phone conversation I'd had with my father just the previous night.

"Dad, you should see this place. It's unbelievable what she's done."

"She only takes kids?"

"Yeah, just kids with life-threatening illnesses."

There was a pause.

"Couldn't you talk her into taking an old man with a bad liver?"

And so my journeys with *The Sporting Life* took me the length and breadth of America, from boardrooms to locker rooms to stables far away, to visit wealthy giants and the downtrodden alike. Somehow, unknowing, I was preparing myself for what was to come in my own life. A smile, a frown, a tear shed, an emotional rainbow that helped make sense of God's creations. One of my favorites came early on, as a world record was about to be broken . . . a record nobody would ever want to claim.

■ OCTOBER 1992

Treboh Joe's bright walnut eyes darted my way that autumn day in 1992 and then dropped, as though he knew he couldn't hide any longer. Willie Mitchell, soft-spoken and gentle, brushed Joe's mane and told him it was okay, didn't matter; they were buddies and winning wasn't the only thing.

"Steady, boy, ain't nobody gonna be embarrassing you. You just stand tall and be proud."

Just looking at this magnificent animal, one would never have guessed that he was anything less than a champion. Even at the age of eleven, his back was ramrod straight, his eyes alert, his step fancy and full of life. What was lacking, then? Was it the heart? Was it the man with the whip in the buggy behind him? Or perhaps he was simply one of those marginal athletes we see on every college campus, even in the professional ranks; athletes with wonderful physical attributes but lacking that one tiny spark that elevates them a notch above.

A truck stood nearby, overflowing with horses, eyes wide in panic, snorting for rescue, ready to be taken to a nearby dog-food factory. Horses that could not run anymore, horses that weren't useful to the racing industry, horses that were taking up valuable stalls, sold by their owners for the price of flesh. (Tell them winning wasn't the only thing.)

No one would take Treboh Joe away, though. Willie would see to it. They were a team—a losing team, mind you, but a team nonetheless. On this particular night at Pocono Downs in eastern Pennsylvania, they would finish out of the money again. Another loss in what had become a staggering number. Treboh Joe, you see, was about to become officially the "losingest" racehorse, harness or thoroughbred, in history. It became 149 straight that night, to grow worse in the months ahead. He had a problem and not one you might imagine. He was just good enough to qualify to race but just bad enough to lose.

"He'd probably be gone from here if he weren't such good copy," said the track public-relations man. "We keep him around as a gimmick, to be honest. Otherwise, he'd be . . . well, somewhere else, for sure."

"Doesn't matter," Willie Mitchell said into the camera, "he's my pal."

A frustrated owner had given Joe to Willie as a Christmas present the year before. No strings, just take him; do something with him. Some present; a living, breathing, grain-consuming present that for sure wasn't going to earn its keep. And so Willie, sleeping in a shed behind Joe's stall to save money, continued to race him—and continued to lose—but never stopped loving him, never stopped whispering good words in his alert ears.

Finally, a year after his story ran on CNN, the horse was retired and adopted by a nearby farm family with children who didn't understand racing charts, and parents who thought a slow horse was just fine.

■ FEBRUARY 1997

From losers to winners . . . and everything in between. The only thing Joe and another *Sporting Life* subject had in common was the number of legs and the color of his mane. Steady Star, instead, had been the world's fastest trotter, breaking the mile mark decades before.

Instead of a child's backyard in his retirement, he had an enormous corral all to himself. Lookout Mountain, near Chattanooga, the site of such bloodshed just a century before, was to his south and when the early-morning mist settled in, you could almost hear the cannon fire and smell the war's anger as the Confederacy held on. Steady Star was thirty years old when I visited him, nearing a hundred in human years, and yet his back was straight and his eyes full of fire. And when they let out the mares in the pasture next to his, he would prance like a teenager, begging for their attention.

"He's just a big ol' kid," laughed Chester Ault, who had owned him forever and had raced him to the monumental world record years before. He was nearly eighty-five and yet, immaculate in suit and tie, he worked every day in his small real-estate office, breaking only to visit his pride and joy. They were growing old together.

"That big ol' horse may never die. He's got too much life in him. Just look!"

Steady Star would stand like a bronzed statue for minutes at a time, ears pricked, as though remembering his calling, and then suddenly bolt across the pasture in an arc that surely was a harness track in his mind. Around he would fly, no carriage to drag him down, circling from right to left just as he had so many times in a long-ago era, to return to where he had stood so erect just minutes before. At attention again, probably for the photographers.

He died two years later, and instead of tears, his passing drew a smile when I heard. An appreciation of a full and glorious life lived far beyond anyone's expectation.

■ JULY 1997

One of the great honors of doing that show was being able to tell the tale of overcoming life's odds, something Chad Yale continues to do even today. It was in the wee hours of a frigid February morning when the train that always brought the dawn to the little North Dakota town derailed behind his family's house. Chad was sixteen years old, a great baseball fan who dreamed of making it to the big leagues one day.

He roused his family, told them what had happened, and he and his father began bundling up to go out and see if they could help. The family car had been plugged in to keep the battery from freezing and the last thing Chad remembers was pulling the plug from the garage

wall. The explosion was the second in minutes to rock the neighborhood, and it nearly left Chad Yale in cinders. Burned over his entire
body, he was given a 1 percent chance of survival by the doctors in
charge. That 1 percent became 10 and then 50, but it was nearly four
months before he was out of the woods completely. Left severely
scarred for life, his right arm gone, he could have given up. But about
that time, one of the players from the local minor-league baseball
team came to visit him in the hospital. They bonded instantly and
Greg Olson, the former Braves catcher, came back many times, visited the family home, and phoned often. And after the railroad gave
Chad a large cash settlement, Olson suggested the young man might
like to buy into the Class A Southern Minny Stars in Austin,
Minnesota, not far away from the Yale home.

"He said he'd think about it," Olson says with a laugh today, "but
that was just to make me sweat. He thought for about five seconds."

And thus Chad Yale became the youngest majority owner in
baseball history. Fate took one dream away and offered another in
return. Ironically, his manager, a twenty-six-year-old named Kevin
Graber, was in the process of overcoming cancer. Together, the two
drew strength from each other while pursuing their great love.

"What did we learn?" Chad's mother voiced the question. "We
live for today. There are no more tomorrows, just todays. Chad
taught us that."

chapter fourteen

like moses in the bulrushes

■ FEBRUARY 1994

The disease that would take my father's life was just beginning to quietly, anonymously awaken from its half-century-old genesis in the spring of '94. No one would realize its presence for another five years, until the damage was already done, so his focus—and mine—remained on the problems of others. We worked almost in unison on the stories of *The Sporting Life*; me in the midst of the fury, he on the other end of a telephone offering his support, hearing the tales, and thanking his God for small blessings. The two of us, and indeed everyone remotely associated with the show, were offered heaping portions of perspective during its run.

Sometimes the challenge was on the outside, sometimes deep within, for our subjects.

Bob Love was a player with the Chicago Bulls in the early '70s. A terrific shooter, he held almost all the Bulls' scoring records until a certain Michael came to town. But Bob Love, who had been called "Butterbean" since his childhood days in Louisiana, never became a full-fledged star because he could hardly talk. He stuttered so badly that no companies came forward for endorsements; no agent was able to turn him into someone you would want to buy a car or even deodorant from. He was a poor, unhappy soul. I recall covering the 1972 NBA All-Star Game in Los Angeles, of which Bob Love was a very deserving member. After practice one morning, the usual throng of writers began moving from one locker to the next, harvesting quotes, when we came to Butterbean's cubicle. Oh, how he tried to talk. He scrunched up his face and tied up his tongue and summoned great forces but nothing would come out. And as the tears began to well in his huge eyes, we slowly moved away, embarrassed, leaving him to the loneliness that had plagued him his entire life.

In the years following his retirement, unable to land a job because of his speech impediment, he wound up in Seattle, washing dishes and busing tables at a large department store's cafeteria.

"Oh, it was so embarrassing," he said to me, picking through the minefield that clutters a stutterer's mouth. "They'd come in for dinner and see me and I'd see them whispering to their wives or to their sons, 'See that guy over there, washing dishes? That's Bob Love. He was an all-star in the NBA and look at him now, busing tables and washing dishes.' It hurt so bad."

But one day, a store executive came to Bob and said they would advance him, but only if he got some therapy (which they paid for). He went from one speech therapist to another, trying everything.

"One of them," he told me, groaning at the memory, "wanted me to go stand on a street corner and say hello to strangers. Now, imagine how that feels."

Finally, he found a woman whose message made sense, and they worked together for the longest of times.

"I had this dream," he said that day of my visit. "I had it often, too, from the time I was just a kid. I was standing in front of this huge crowd and I was speaking to the people . . . like Dr. King or John Kennedy. I wasn't stuttering; I was speaking plain and good, and the crowd was loving it. Oh, I hated to wake up from that dream because when I did, I was back stuttering."

Bob Love stands before those crowds now, speaking as the Bulls' director of community relations. Hundreds of times a year, boldly, proudly, and charismatically, he tells them his story, and if there are children in the audience, he makes certain they know that *anything* is possible. He walks the sidelines during home games, meeting and greeting, a huge smile across his handsome face.

"Imagine me in front of a crowd." He laughed that day. Imagine indeed.

My father loved Butterbean Love's story. He knew a thing or two about a stuttering life.

He never admitted it to my mother, but he also liked another of our *Sporting Life* characters, one who wasn't down-and-out or sad or disabled, but simply one of life's engaging people. (We had plenty of those too.)

"Tell me the truth," he half-whispered one day after the story of Morgana ran, "did she kiss your cheek too?"

■ NOVEMBER 1992

In fact, she did. The Great Kissing Bandit made a habit of that in those days. She had leaped onto baseball fields and basketball courts for years, her voluptuous figure drawing immediate attention from players and fans alike. And with great ceremony, as the crowd roared its appreciation, she would reach up and kiss the star player on the cheek. As the player would redden and laugh her away, the police would good-naturedly lead her off the field so she could plot her next adventure.

I didn't know what to expect when we arrived at the doorstep of her modest Columbus, Ohio, home that spring day. I had talked to her by phone several times to set up the interview but, having seen her act, wondered what she would be like in person. It didn't take long to find out.

With one ring of the doorbell, she flung the door open, greeted me and my cameraman with identical Easter baskets filled with the stuff of her "career"—trading cards, a magazine, signed pictures.

"Y'all come on in," she said with a laugh. And thus began one of the most unexpectedly delightful days I've ever enjoyed. She slaved over a hot stove cooking us lunch and served us on the screened-in back porch. Sitting quietly nearby was her husband, a bespectacled, balding career college student who had helped engineer all of her kissing stunts over the years.

"I'd be back in the shadows." He laughed, remembering their exploits.

"But he'd be right there," she quickly joined in, "to bail me out."

It was a curious career, one that made her a household name in many sports houses and one she took into midlife. Though I never asked her age, just simple deduction would have made her, um, let's just say . . . mature. But one of the kindest, nicest, sweetest bandits I've ever met.

It wasn't the usual *Sporting Life* story, but it was one that brought forth the usual envy from my peers.

"You lead a tough life, Huber," my friends and coworkers would tease me. "Got any room in the suitcase for when you do the sequel? I'd like to come along."

We very intentionally brought out every human emotion each

month, be it anger or sadness, fear or laughter. The show's original charter was to explore humanity's spirit, to showcase those brave souls who challenge life's odds. Throughout the decade, we accomplished our goal, and it took only minimal searches to find them. They were everywhere; not always in the headlines, but sometimes buried deep within the subtext, or sometimes not even worth a mention at all . . . to those who chose not to look close enough.

■ APRIL 1993

Ferguson Jenkins ranked with the former. He had a record six straight twenty-win seasons for the Chicago Cubs—which was like driving a horse and buggy to a half dozen Daytona 500 championships in a row. The Cubs were so mediocre he often won *in spite* of them. And in the midst of that incredible run of seasons, his mother died of stomach cancer. It was only the first of life's many slaps upside this man's fine head.

He and his young stepson, Raymond, lived alone on a 160-acre ranch outside Guthrie, Oklahoma, when the *Sporting Life* paid a call. His hair was speckled with gray, his eyes sad and bloodshot, his once-powerful shoulders stooped. He and Raymond worked the ranch together, taking care of the cattle, making sure life maintained its balance. But if it hadn't been for the boy, I had the feeling Fergie Jenkins might have just faded into the sunset. He and his wife, Mary Ann, Raymond's mother, had found this wonderful sprawling spread in 1990.

"She just took one look at it," Fergie remembered, "and said, 'This is it, we look no more.' She just loved it here."

They added a daughter, Samantha, to the ranch's roster, and life was grand.

But one night, as Mary Ann came home from her job with a

local car dealership, she lost control on a seemingly harmless stretch of highway not ten miles from the ranch, and her car flipped three times.

"Doctors said she wouldn't last the night," the old pitcher recalled, his eyes flooding. "But she lasted thirty-five days, somehow struggling and fighting to live."

On the day after her husband was elected to the Baseball Hall of Fame (on the third try), as he read the clippings so proudly to her and saw her smile, she died of pneumonia. She was just days shy of thirty-two years old.

A friend of Mary Ann's was one of the caring people who came by the ranch to pay their respects. She offered to help with baby Samantha. In time, Fergie and Cynthia found solace in each other.

"But she was sick, as it turns out," he said quietly the day we talked. "One day, she took the baby, got into the car, started the engine, and committed suicide. Samantha died too. Oh . . ."

His voice caught and his eyes lowered. "She left a note, said she was sorry she had to take Samantha with her, but didn't want her to be alone."

The loss of three women in his life within such a short period of time tore through the old right-hander's insides. Coincidentally, he had purchased two burial plots (two for the price of one) when Mary Ann had died and now both were filled, with an additional small one nearby.

If it's true that the good Lord doesn't give a man any more than he can handle, then Ferguson Jenkins was either a second Job or he was at the last threads of a long, fraying rope. The loss of his daughter still gets to him.

"I can't see a little girl without breaking up," he admits. "I remember being in an airport gate one day and this woman came up with a beautiful baby girl and I just had to leave. I couldn't even board the plane. I just walked away and got on the next one. It hurts so much."

I would see Fergie Jenkins here and there in the years after the story ran, after he slowly got back into baseball, and he always had a smile, always a friendly handshake. He talked once about another wife and I silently prayed that this one would last, that the man deserved no more pain. I saw how he had handled death—not particularly well, yet with a certain dignity—and I remember wondering how we are equipped for such an eventuality. Fergie poured himself into his son, worked the ranch with a vengeance, found a corner in the big ranch house that he and Mary Ann had designed themselves, and sat there until the tears dried up. He did not walk life's streets in search of sympathy. In fact, the dirt road to the ranch needed a specific set of directions to find. It was his shrine and his hideout. I wondered how I would handle such setbacks, God forbid.

■ FEBRUARY 1994

The most arduous—and the proudest—undertaking of the 190 tales we told on *The Sporting Life* over the years came during the midst of the Yugoslav rebellion. We heard whispers that two coaches had managed to somehow sneak the entire Yugoslav junior Olympic basketball team out of the country, in the dead of night under enemy fire, children fleeing for their lives, trying to save their futures and indeed the future of basketball in that once-proud country. Their families gave their blessings, glad to know their boys were going to be safe for the weeks or months this conflict would last. Surely it would not linger any longer than that.

"Sorta like Moses hidden in the bulrushes," said the lawyer who helped, "sent floating down the Nile to safety."

Through a convoluted set of circumstances, crossing an airport tarmac under heavy gunfire in the dead of night, going first to Greece and then to Germany, the entire team was finally relocated to the suburbs of Chicago, one here, one there, no two together. Families adopted them for the moment and helped them integrate into their individual school systems. After all, it wouldn't have been fair to simply deposit these talented young athletes all in one high school. So they spread out across the lush, green countryside. Their own families had no knowledge of their whereabouts or their safety, and could only pray.

One November night near Thanksgiving in 1993, we managed to gather the boys all together in a church hall. While their temporary parents huddled at one end to compare notes—who was doing well, who was struggling, who was homesick, who was benefiting from the change—the boys joined arms at the other end, singing old folk songs in a language they hadn't used in months, laughing as they hadn't in years; together again, if only for one night.

To say the entire operation had been difficult would have been the understatement of the year. Who were the greater heroes, the frightened young boys ducking bullets on their way to temporary freedom, or the families, interrupting their safe and secure lifestyles to take in these youngsters? Most of the boys knew some English (it was required in their schools back home), but it was stilted and embarrassing for them and they struggled. Though they became instant paladins to their new schoolmates as they slipped immediately into starring roles on their new high school basketball teams, most of them remained terribly lonely.

"I feel," one surrogate mother told me, "kinda like I have a new son. But I'm one of the lucky ones. I know he has a mother back in Yugoslavia; I correspond with her as much as possible to let her know he's doing okay. And I know he misses her very much. I hear him crying at night in his room."

After all, they were still children, victims of grown-up politics.

One by one that cold autumn night, we called them to sit in a separate room before our camera and, in their native tongue, send whatever message they wanted to their parents. We would deliver video postcards. One by one, the athletic machismo melted away, and through the tears, they told their mothers and fathers they were okay, they loved them, and they hoped they would all be back together again soon.

After the first two boys came and went, we looked at each other through tears and said, "That's probably enough." We hadn't understood a word they had said, but we had understood every heartbeat.

Jim Minnehan—the lawyer who had helped bring them all to Illinois, who had talked doctors into giving them examinations, dentists into working on terrible decay, merchants into shoeing them and putting clothes on their backs—looked back at us and smiled.

"Oh, no, you're not getting away that easy. They all want to talk to their parents."

And so, one by one, large and small, they took their seat and spilled their emotional guts. In the first few seconds, they would seem embarrassed and shy, not knowing what to say. And then, remembering their purpose, they would tumble headlong into magical and moving monologues.

Our Sarajevo "bureau" as it were—just a cameraman and a producer—took time away from the war and found as many of the boys' parents as possible, brought them separately to our small office and, on some of the only generated electricity left in the city, showed them their sons on a small television monitor. One mother had lost a leg to a sniper. Another had lost her husband. They quickly forgot their own problems, for they watched boys who were children no longer and stifled great sobs as they heard the messages.

"Oh, look," one mother cried, "he's a foot taller! He's become a man."

She watched her son walk through his new school's hallways, a full head taller than most of his classmates. She watched him running onto the basketball court, framed by an enormous American flag hanging on one wall. She watched his sad eyes, red and full of tears, as he gathered his feelings and spilled them out to her in his Slavic tongue. Suddenly, her leg did not hurt anymore; it was her heart that ached.

We then allowed the parents to return the greetings and took that video back to Illinois for the boys to see. They talked of the war, of the gutted buildings around which many of the boys had once played, of their younger brothers and sisters, of their prayers. Once again, I needed no interpreter to understand their emotions.

It was called "the Moses Project."

They were just tall athletic children and yet far older than their years, hardened by the curious war that had torn their homeland apart. Bosnians and Serbs alike, Christians and Muslims, they understood very little of the religious politics that had forced them away.

"It makes no sense," one sixteen-year-old told me in his stilted English. "Sarajevo was once a beautiful city. Now it is blown apart . . . for what? Nobody can explain to me for what."

He shrugged his sturdy shoulders and stifled a tear. Those would come later, in a torrent, as he abandoned his hardened teenage bravado and watched the video postcard from his mother, her weary eyes dark and troubled, but so happy for that single moment to have contact. He may have been old beyond his years, but a child's heart still beat in his chest and he and his comrades were homesick for a land that would never be again.

It was a story with a mixed climax. Some of their real parents were able to come to the United States to visit their sons. Others remained behind, never knowing. The boys graduated. Some went on to college on athletic scholarships, to Syracuse and Tennessee-Chattanooga. Others remained alone.

It was a story . . . and yet so much more. It took months of effort on the part of a terrific producer named Robert Abbott and our bureaus, a coordination that was built around dedication not simply to our business, but to these young men. Everyone who worked on the Moses Project seemed to become part of a wonderful expedition into the human spirit. We ventured past the journalistic cutoff point and became a part of the story, wanting these boys to succeed, wanting their real parents to find them, wanting their surrogate families to feel proud of the sacrifices. It was one time when roaming across that age-old line of "not getting involved" didn't matter one bit.

chapter fifteen

pieces of life's puzzle

"I worry about you," my mother told me one night long-distance.

"Why in the world . . . ?"

"Are you wearing yourself out with all these sad stories?" she asked. "You seem to make them a part of your life, and I don't know if that's real healthy."

She most likely had a point; she usually did. It was one reason why we clashed so often, cut from the very same cloth were we. She always looked much younger than her age, so when I was a teenager people asked her if I was her brother. She loved that, but didn't particularly care for the emotional wrestling that came with that territory. We thought alike, had the same approach to life, and neither of us liked hearing the truth so often. We fought often, and even today, we both know what will raise the bristles on the other's back. When I was younger, I almost took delight in pushing the right buttons, but now, just the thought of drawing tears, such a sad look overtaking that wonderful face, usually gives me pause. Usually.

"Oh, Mom, I'm fine. You worry too much."

But, as always, she was right. Why in the world was I putting myself through this monthly fight-to-the-death with the devil? Dad seemed to understand but never said much.

"You okay?" he would ask.

"Sure, why?"

"Oh, I don't know. Just wondering." I knew my mother had inspired the question, but he seemed satisfied with the answer. Perhaps we had more in common than either of us ever believed.

The range of subjects over the decade that *The Sporting Life* ran on CNN covered a hundred years of life, but it was those at either end of the spectrum who usually provided the most emotion. Children seemed to hit us the hardest. Pitcher Bryan Harvey's daughter had Happy Puppet Syndrome, which kept her from flexing her arms and legs. Quarterback Doug Flutie's son Dougie was autistic. Former Cy Young winner Steve Bedrosian and his wife Tammy's son Cody had leukemia, and battled it through one remission and into another. Lauren Reynolds had brittle-bone disease, but still won swimming ribbons, competed in wheelchair races, and made it to the Sydney Paralympic Games.

■ SEPTEMBER 1995

And then there was Amy White.

The oldest daughter of Ed and Joan White, she was a cheerleader and the homecoming queen, and she was headed for college on a basketball scholarship. Her father was the former all-pro offensive guard with the Vikings and Chargers; a huge but very gentle man given to tremendous torment, for his baby was dying.

On the evening before her parents' twenty-fifth wedding anniversary, Amy and some friends went out to buy some flowers. The arrangement was too big to fit in the car so Amy volunteered to open the hatchback and sit back there as they drove across the parking lot to an ice-cream shop. It wasn't more than two hundred yards and the car was traveling no more than ten miles an hour when it hit the speed bump. Amy fell backward, her head striking the pavement. She remained in a coma for nearly two years. They brought her home, set up a special room, hired therapists and nurses, and spent hours of loving time with her each day.

The day I was there in San Diego with a crew, Ed took me to her room and introduced me, as though he were interrupting her homework. He leaned over her and kissed her forehead. Her eyes were open but never moved. He whispered something sweet, smiled and kissed her again.

You could read the pain on his and Joan's faces clearly; it never left. Ed was coaching the offensive line at San Diego State University and his players told me they often saw the ravages of his misery. Any other coach, they might have rebelled. But they all knew Amy, too; they were a part of her family and understood.

Somehow they coped—and would continue for as long as it took. "She'll come back to us one day," Ed said. "I just know she will."

But she didn't. Three years later, she finally died. Someone sent me a clipping from a San Diego newspaper and I sought my usual dark corner for a moment, not for Amy but for Ed and Joan.

They live and they die. They suffer and they triumph.

As I did these stories—as I researched and then did the interviews, as I sat down and reviewed the tape, as I wrote the final piece—I slowly became aware of small pieces being added to my life's puzzle. Of what it must have been like to have been my parents, struggling; of what it must have been like, facing death. Each story almost invariably brought me to a closer understanding of not only *their* lives, but mine too. I would rush home and sit for hours, sharing either the joy or the tears of the marvel I had just witnessed. And then I would pick up the phone and repeat the process with my family. They saw (in her husband, in their son) a not-so-subtle change. I was becoming more appreciative of my life, of their being in it, of having had so many gifts given. It happened slowly, for I was wont to abandon that hardened, brassy image of the sportscaster, but they could feel the rough edges smooth and the furrowed brow relax.

And then I would dive headfirst into one more.

■ JUNE 1998

The little boy was just six years old when he ran in front of the thundering semi-tractor trailer on a busy rural road in Utah.

"I watched in horror," his mother told me, "and suddenly all I saw were little legs twisting around the huge tires. I knew he was dead."

He lost one of those legs on the scene; another would last only until the life-flight got him to the nearest trauma center. They amputated at the pelvis and thus he wasn't even left with stumps. But they didn't take his heart, and slowly he found his way back.

Like so many children faced with adversity, he adapted to life without legs, scurrying along the ground on his hands as he played ball, balancing on the kitchen counter as he made his lunch. There was a wheelchair and there were crutches but they seemed lost in his dust, so anxious was he to get from here to there. He was eleven when we visited, and every sequence of his life left indelible images. Getting up before dawn, running fingers through that thick red mop of hair, he would climb into the wheelchair to deliver the morning newspapers. It was a manual chair and the hills he had to climb were steep and torturous, but he never complained. At school he worked his way through gym class with all the rest of the kids, doing handstands and push-ups and practically everything everybody else was asked to do.

In the afternoon after school, out of the chair and onto his pelvis, he played basketball with some buddies in the neighborhood cul-de-sac.

But the image that will remain with me forever came on the weekend as he played a Little League baseball game, not in a league for disabled kids—which would have been entirely appropriate—but with able-bodied teammates. He played right field and darned if he didn't scramble after one ball and throw out an opponent at second base. Why, you'd have thought he'd just won the World Series, the cry of joy was that loud. He took his turn hitting, just a regular kid dragging himself and a bat to the plate. Opposing pitchers had a tough time finding his strike zone for, realistically, it was nowhere near what they were used to facing, and so he walked several times. He even scored a run once as his team won. And when it was over, he and his friends celebrated their victory and made their way home. It was our final view of him, arm in arm with a pal, going back over every wonderful play they'd made, looking off into the Pacific sunset.

I had many wonderful editors work on my stories over the years but one of my favorites was Peggy Kearney, a brash little woman from Long Island who was all bark. She would fuss and fret and worry as she wrestled with the elaborate process of editing a piece, but in the end, would offer a hug and a thank-you.

I grew to love the entire process of putting a story together, from the original investigation to the shooting to sitting in that tiny booth with an editor for hours as she lay down shot after shot, picking the right music, letting it breathe, giving it a kind of life. Editing is a wonderful, inventive, collaborative art. Some editors like to take a script and your raw video and simply close the door and work alone, painting the picture precisely where you put the numbers. Others enjoy the joint effort, knowing how much of ourselves we often put into every story.

We would gather steam together, feeding off each other, sharing ideas, arguing style and substance but never soul. When I worked local television, I learned to edit my stories by myself. There was no union; thus I was free to sit and create all alone. But at the network, the process became more elaborate and complicated, and trained editors were essential. When you got a good editor—and we had many—the final three or four hours of a story could be as invigorating and energizing as anything else you could do.

In the middle of putting this story together, after looking at hours of tape of the young man and his valiant struggle, Peggy turned to me and simply said: "Next time I complain about anything . . . anything at all . . . kick me, will you?"

Our stories had that kind of effect on almost everyone involved. They offered perspective and drew tears and made us all aware that our world wasn't completely bad, that there were good tales out there to be told. I was fortunate, for I was allowed to spend most of my time in pursuit of such marvels, and it seemed to be one reason why so many editors enjoyed the respite of working on my pieces. Their days and nights were taken up, as were the reporters' and anchors', with the mundane constants of sport. If I grew weary of telling the nightly tale of the home run and the three-point field goal, imagine the editors who have to piece those highlights together each night, game after game. To be able to wander through these lives, if for just a few hours, breathed new life into their days.

■ OCTOBER 1995

Was it God's will or simply the convergence of the moon and stars? It is probably best not to question the great coincidences of life, but to simply accept them, appreciate them, be in awe of them . . . and hope for more.

Gary and Sheryl Waldman lived a meager life in a small Iowa town called Correctionville and when she gave birth to a very premature baby girl years ago, they saw immediately that their prayers for a healthy child had gone unanswered. The little girl was so sick that doctors finally agreed to take her off the ventilator. Gary was holding her tiny hand as they began unhooking the wires. Suddenly, he felt her grip tighten. And she held on to his finger for dear life.

"I looked down and saw her take a deep breath," he remembers now, "and I made a commitment to her that very moment, that if she was willing to fight that hard for life, I would do everything in my power to make it as good a life as possible."

She survived the first few tests but would settle into a series of distressing problems. Suffering from seizure disorder and cerebral palsy, she could not begin to function on her own. And the Waldmans, woefully in debt, could not keep up. So the state took this girl they named Serena and put her in a state-supported home called the Faith, Hope and Charity Home for Special Children.

When Serena was two, she was allowed to go for a ride in a hot-air balloon, and as her father described it, she soared skyward with the balloon, like a tiny bird. He saw what brought her joy and wondered how other disabled children would react. They would first need a balloon and then one with a handicap gate—not a common thing. And so he and some friends built one; held bake sales, raffles, and auctions to raise money to build and fly this great balloon they would call Serena's Song. It would not only serve Serena herself, but as many other disabled children as they could reach across the Midwest.

Two thousand miles to the west, a wealthy older couple named Bob and Beverly Lewis, who were in the business of racing horses, bought a wonderful filly and trained it with their eyes on the Triple Crown.

"But what do we name her?" Bob recalls. "Beverly got a book of names out and finally said, 'Well, what do you think about Serena?'

"I said I thought that was a very nice and proper name for such a lovely filly as this. And she said, 'What about Serena's Song?' And so it was."

As Serena's Song (the horse) began to make national headlines, racing its way toward Churchill Downs and the Kentucky Derby, Gary Waldman read the stories and saw the irony. He contacted Bob Lewis and told him of his dream for the balloon but that he had no money. Bob, who had long sponsored a home for disabled adults, was instantly enthralled and promised Gary a healthy donation from every race his horse ran during her three-year-old career, the prime of her national exposure.

And together, though hundreds of miles apart, the two Serena's Songs flew like the wind. Children's laughter filled the sky; adults' cheers filled the grandstands. It was one of the most improbable and yet perfectly understandable unions ever.

"I feel like a meadowlark sitting on a fencepost here in the middle of Iowa," Gary said. "Only one song to sing but I sing it and sing it and sing it until somebody can hear and make a difference."

■ JANUARY 1997

I didn't connect my parents directly to many of my *Sporting Life* subjects until the early moments of 1997 when I went to south Florida to tell the story of Joanne Carner and Judy Dickinson. Both were legends on the Ladies Professional Golf Association tour. Carner was always "Big Mama" and Dickinson was president of the players association and a force within the tour. But both were now struggling with life's bogeys.

Joanne and her husband, Don, had traveled the tour for a quarter century, fixtures at every stop. He was her guiding light, her shield and protector, and the love of her life. But now he was settling into dementia, a sad state that was slowly taking him away from her. When she played the tour—and that was becoming more rare by the year—she had to find someone to take care of him. Sometimes an adult day-care center was the answer. Other times, friends would watch him while she played.

"It's so sad," she said in her gruff, cigarette-stoked voice. "We were always together, everywhere, and now . . . well, sometimes he knows me and sometimes he just goes away somewhere, deep inside himself."

Ten miles up the interstate, Judy Dickinson lived with her twin sons and husband, Gardner, a golf legend in his own right. A wonderful player and then a great teacher of the game, he was not only Judy's love but her life. A late marriage for both of them, it was full of wonder and delight. He not only helped Judy with her game but worked with Joanne as well. But a stroke had debilitated him and now he could only sit and watch and wonder.

"He has a tough time getting around," she told me that day, Joanne sitting next to her at the kitchen table. "He sits in his wheelchair and watches the boys play football in the front yard and you can see that urge in his eyes to get out there with them. But he can't.

"It's tough on the boys too. I think they understand but I don't know."

While I stood by Gardner's chair that day and watched the rough-and-tumble world of the eight-year-olds, and Don Carner sat alone in the car, Judy and Joanne slowly walked through the backyard. Dozens of orange trees heavy with fruit gave them cover from the January sun. They gained sustenance from each other, comparing notes on the balance between good days and bad, wondering what the future would hold. They had shared so much of the LPGA's heritage over the last few decades and were now sharing something deeper and painful.

"Sorta makes a bad round of golf seem not so important, y'know?" Carner said. "Thought we'd be young and foolish forever. Doesn't work that way, I guess."

I thought of my parents and how fortunate they were. Older by a decade than either of these couples and still rich with life and health, able to huddle together and survive most anything.

Or so I thought then.

chapter sixteen

the final hours

■ OCTOBER 1999

Dad looked upset. It was just two weeks before his death.

"What's wrong?" I asked.

"Clowns," he returned. "Clowns were just here and they pulled up my shirt"—he feebly pointed to where a nurse had installed a catheter that morning—"and they painted me red down there."

"Good clowns or bad clowns? Were they happy or being devilish?"

"I never asked. I'm just upset about the paint. I'm all red."

With every breath possibly his last, we lingered close, watching. One night, I drew sleep-in duty, pulling out the sofa bed and spending the night, to help if anything went wrong. To be there. Sleep was nearly impossible for one ear was always pricked to any sounds coming from their bedroom. The first few hours were uneventful, underlined by the comfort of a steady, soft snore. Suddenly out of the darkness, down the hallway, I heard him say something. I jumped up and rushed to his side.

"Trucks," he mumbled, still asleep. He took a huge breath and it seemed an hour before he let it out again. I went back to my bed thinking how twisted it would be if the man's last word on earth would be *trucks*. (It would turn out to be much worse. As it happened, his final sentence on earth was, "I'd like a pickle." Perhaps it was simply his own punch line.)

A night later, my mother, my brother, and I were together in the waning hours of another disconsolate day. We had talked ourselves out and so we sat silently lost in our thoughts when we heard him call my name. We hurried down the hallway, his old path to heaven. Had it been only a few weeks since he'd actually made that journey with his walker?

We surrounded his bed as he looked at us, one by one. It was as though he had been lying there, preparing a speech in his mind. It was so formal. In the darkness, with only the echo of light from the hallway, he began.

"Jim, I wanna thank you for all you've done and for being a good son," he said slowly, "and I want you to have something." He asked my mother to get a small mahogany box out of a special drawer in his nearby chest where he kept his "things." In the box were a gleaming pocket watch and penknife. With trembling hands, he held it out for me to take.

"And Chuck, I wanna thank you for everything, too, and I want you to have my tool kit, the one out in the kitchen. I love you both very, very much."

And the man joined us all, sobbing. Though it had become a ritual between him and my mother, I had never seen him cry in all our years.

"Is it time?" my mother asked.

"Go in peace," my brother said.

"It's okay, Dad," I added. "We know you have to leave us."

Another good-bye, but surely this was the last. It was choreographed like a movie. There should have been music, soft and gripping, in the background.

He asked for a tissue, took his time wiping the tears away. He worked the tissue as he always had the wrapping on a gift, infuriatingly slow so as to never rip or spoil it. He was one of those who refused to tear open a present.

It became one of his holiday trademarks and he would sit and take forever, to the impatient chagrin of us all, patiently peeling off the tape and carefully unwrapping what had been given him. The more we urged him to just rip it, the longer he took. And that night he seemed to be playing the tissue the same way.

One last reminder of times gone by.

We were in awe, watching this play out. It was surely the end. We each touched him in the darkness. Together, we said the Lord's Prayer. I could hear him keeping up:

"Deliver us from evil, for thine is the kingdom."

He gasped and his chest grew large with air. A minute, maybe two, later, he let it out.

"You're wetting me," he said to my mother, whose tears had been falling on his arm.

We looked at each other. What was this?

"Oh," he moaned, "I don't remember the last time I was this emotional. It was . . ."

I thought perhaps it might have been just three weeks earlier when he had attended his granddaughter's wedding, had actually sat up front in his wheelchair, had let her sit in his lap for pictures when it was over. Just three weeks ago! He had dissolved so quickly since then.

"At Nan's wedding?" I prompted.

"No . . ."

"At your own wedding?"

"No . . ."

And he paused for the longest time, letting the drama unfold.

". . . when Grandma ran over the cat."

I asked him the next morning what in the world he had meant by that. He shook his head slowly and chuckled.

"You all were so serious," he said. "I just wanted to lighten things up."

There is always a rush to bring sainthood to the dying, to make them far larger in death than in life. And so it was with my father and me. I scurried through my memories to somehow inspire what he meant to me. What grand lessons I took from him. My debt. But another man, a neighbor, taught me how to throw a fastball and how to not be afraid on the receiving end of one. A friend took me through the jump shot and another how to pass a spiral. Dad was far too busy trying to support the family to have time for such trivial endeavors.

When he wasn't working, it was worse. During the summer before my first-grade year, he was in traction in an upstairs bed recovering from back surgery. They thought he had broken his back during the war, somewhere in the waters of the South Pacific. But he never felt it and came home to begin the rest of his life. One day, walking on his way to business school, he blacked out and doctors discovered the break. His back would forever plague him and eventually force him into early retirement. And the original surgery demanded the transfusion that eventually killed him nearly fifty years later. But in the spring of 1950, he was simply laid up for a month, flat on his back, out of our lives, either sleeping all day or reading the projection of a book onto the ceiling overhead.

My friends all had fathers they could produce, fathers who did things with them. I had an invalid that year, and so one day when my first-grade buddies pressed me on the issue, I told them that my father was Hopalong Cassidy and that he was off fighting bad guys. For some reason (perhaps this was my storytelling genesis) they believed me and I was a hero for a while until I had to produce the great Hollywood cowboy or get beat up. I obviously got whaled and I'm sure a short session on a couch would make great hay of such a life-changing moment.

My Hopalong got better and went back to work, not fighting bad guys, but selling insurance or delivering bread or directing traffic at that point.

So even when I finally could produce him for my pals to see, it was only at a distance. We never once played ball. (I wonder today if he even knew how.) He did teach me the proper way of inserting an electric prong in the ground so night crawlers would come scurrying to the surface, bait for a fishing excursion to the nearby lake. But I never had the patience for either that or the fishing. He tried to get me under the hood of the '55 Buick but my brother seemed better suited to mechanics.

And, oh yes, "The Talk."

I was thirteen and had already been around the locker room a few times when he closed the door to my bedroom one afternoon, sat me down, and gave me his lecture.

"Thirty seconds of fun," he said, nervously, only doing what my mother had asked that he do, "is not worth a lifetime of sorrow."

And with that, as I was pondering the thirty seconds, he got up, wagged his finger at me, and left the room. Strangely, as I think back over the thousands of days together as father and young son, those are the only words I can recall, the only conversation that has stuck . . . those, and my argument with him over whether Ringo Starr or Buddy Rich was the better drummer. (It wasn't much of a fight. He said Rich and I nodded, turning away to watch the *Ed Sullivan Show*.)

We never, ever fought. Perhaps it's a father-son thing. I fought with my mother constantly, was in her face as often as she was in mine. When we think back on it, the two of us, we shudder at the love we wasted along the way. But I never once had a serious disagreement with my father, which might have underlined our early relationship, what there was of it. He didn't fuss and I worried about what was simmering deep within.

In fact, in all the years together, I can remember just one ugly turn. Of course, it came on account of something I had said to his wife, my mother. We had had a strained telephone conversation that night, about something no longer important. She had, as she was wont to do, fallen into a fit of tears and we had left it that way. It happened occasionally and I hated it, for I felt like the ultimate villain and I meant no original harm, meant only to remind her that I was an adult, too, and had an opinion.

It wasn't a minute later and the phone rang. My father's voice, which was strange, for he rarely placed the call. He always came on in relief. But this time, he was the starter and it wasn't pretty.

"You made your mother cry," he said matter-of-factly.

He wasn't angry, wasn't shouting, and wasn't threatening. He simply wanted me to know my place and to know that I had hurt the woman he loved.

"Sorry, Dad," I quickly said. "I didn't mean it. You know that."

"Yeah, but does she?"

"I think if she considers it long and hard, she knows. I don't mean to be ugly but this isn't the first time. We just have, well, you know, that sort of relationship."

"Try not to make her cry, will you?"

He knew something about that. If I learned anything growing up from the man, it was how to nurture women. He was always a ladies' man, in the best sense of the phrase, gracious and respectful and full of subtle charm. I can only remember him and my mother fighting seriously once. I was very small and it was loud and ugly, doors slamming and tears flowing. It was probably about money. And he handled it as he handled her all his life, by closing down. He was the one who slammed the door, behind him, to go cool off. Strange, the memories, for I couldn't have been older than four or five, but they stuck firm and stark.

In the years to come, he didn't walk out; he just shut down. The fire of her red hair would be billowing about something or other, him just ignoring her. And it only stoked the blaze and made it roar more fiercely. Occasionally, if I happened to be around, he would raise an eye from whatever he was reading, look at me, and wink. He seemed to be enjoying the game, though the pots and pans in the kitchen nearby were rattling madly in protest. Soon, they would have forgotten it all, their makeup done in a private place, if at all.

In the later years, as adults together, the words came easier for him and me, words gradually filled with mutual respect and love. As we merged into a friendship, we found what we had—and didn't have—in common. He laughed at my inability to do simple household chores like installing a rheostat or building a workbench. But he silently relished being needed.

"I wanna build a little workshop in the basement," I told him long ago.

"Why in the world would you want something like that?" He laughed, sure that it would only draw dust.

"I don't know. I guess it's time I learned to do hammer-and-nails kinda stuff."

"You want a workbench then?"

"I guess so."

"We'll need lumber. You have any lumber?" he asked.

"No."

"How about tools?"

"Tools?"

"Yeah, you know, hammers and wrenches and nails and stuff."

"I dunno. Lemme check. I think there's a hammer somewhere."

He would send me in search of this kind of pliers or that kind of screwdriver and invariably I would return with something nowhere near what he had in mind. A Phillips head or a needle-nose seemed to me the stuff of Dr. Seuss.

"Won't this one work just as well?" I would lamely beg. And he would just look at me with a half-chuckle on his face and go find the right tool himself. His father, the machinist, had raised him in their basement tool shop, had taught him how everything worked and why. Unlike me, Dad seemed to absorb the lessons easily. Many of the tools my father kept in his rusty old box had belonged to *his* father, bequeathed as family heirlooms, and my father would gently unwrap them from their cloth shelter and show me.

"Ah, this is probably seventy-five years old," he would muse, "but it's just as good as the ones they make today. Look how sharp . . ."

Uh-huh.

We merrily groaned often about our projects. It became our modus operandi. We would spend days and days building something in the basement, out in the garage, in the backyard, only to reach the final moment of putting it together and discover we had done one thing backward. I often harbored a thought that he did it on purpose, to make the project last a little longer. If it had just been me alone, I would have easily understood the reasons. Idiocy, for one; idiocy and incompetence. But us working together? We had probably been laughing too hard to notice. The laughter, easy and free and joyous, was as much a part of our reborn relationship as anything palpable.

"We never fail," he would say with a chuckle, "to screw up something, do we?"

"Yeah, but we also never fail to have a great time," I'd respond. "And in the end, it works somehow."

He always came to the house prepared, knowing that even if there wasn't a project to complete, he would have chores waiting.

"You want me to bring my tool kit?" he would ask, knowing the answer was always, "Yes."

And so while I got the pocket watch, my brother got that tool kit. Dad knew, even in the end, where our aptitudes remained.

The afternoon was dark and brooding, the bedroom shades drawn as usual.

"Is there anything I can do for you?" my mother asked, leaning over the man she had loved for half a century, just a shell of his body left but the heart still beating nicely.

"Come," said the old man, teeth still in a drawer, "lie down beside me for a while."

Alone in the darkness, they quietly cried.

chapter seventeen

communion in heaven?

He lingered far beyond the most optimistic predictions. Counting the days, we were well into triple figures.

"I don't mean this to be harsh or cruel," wrote my brother mid-summer, "but I can't wait to find out how this turns out. The suspense is killing me."

Nobody knew and everybody guessed. He would be gone by early June, surely by July, couldn't possibly last until the wedding Labor Day weekend. And now here he was again, still keeping us all in the dark. On that September Sunday, as he watched bits and pieces of America's televised comeback victory in the Ryder Cup, doctors realized everything was coming to an end and decided to take him off all medication and solid food. (There is no correlation between the viewing of the Ryder Cup and the decision to let him die, simply a reference of time. He regaled one fondly and cared nothing about the latter.) It was one of the defining moments, as much as the first letting of blood, the selling of the family car, or the calling of Hospice. It was the doctors' way of shutting the door.

He had demanded a living will, insisted that there be no life support, no tubes or wires attached. No heroics.

For some reason, though he had never played the game in his life, he and my mother were ardent golf fans. He didn't watch much football, never baseball, but hardly missed his golf. It is somewhat surprising, then, that his dreams centered on pickup trucks so often and not golf carts, that the angels were coming for him and not Greg Norman. It would be appropriate that the Ryder Cup telecast would be one of the last things he would pay any attention to.

That no more food would be offered drew only a halfhearted shrug.

"Aren't you hungry?"

"Nah. Kinda thirsty, though. Boy, Leonard's putt was a great one, wasn't it?"

And someone put the bent straw to his lips and he took just a sip, no more.

Along that final fortnight, as his body slowly turned itself off, some rearranging magically happened. When they removed his teeth, they also took out his hearing aids. Yet he heard better than he had in decades. They took him off the heart medication that supposedly had been imperative for years, yet he showed no ill effects without it. He had worn glasses forever, it seemed to me, yet, with them sitting near his teeth and his hearing aids in a drawer by the bed, he saw and heard things the rest of us could not.

As the hours ticked away, he thought more and more about his final destination. It became all-consuming. Their minister stopped by often, usually for nothing more than a chat. One afternoon, he brought Dad Communion.

"Will they have Communion in heaven?" Dad asked, quite serious.

The minister, a wonderful young father of twins, thought carefully. "I've never been asked that question before. Let me think for a minute."

They sat together in silence for a second or two.

"Why, how silly," said the minister suddenly, "I don't know why I had to think about it. Of course there won't be Communion because you'll be feasting at the table of God every meal."

Dad looked at him and nodded. Of course.

"It's not Dad anymore," Chuck said. "I don't know who it is, but it's not him."

I had finally given in and gone home, back to work after spending a week there, convinced he would live to be 110. But seconds after I left, he told my mother he knew he would never see me again. And he fell rapidly to the next plateau.

"I almost don't recognize him," my mother said on the phone. "He's not the same."

They held their vigil and watched him slip away. The weeks of good humor and bright dreams, the visions of heaven, were either gone forever or imprisoned within as his words turned to babble. The poison that would have filtered through a healthy liver and kidneys had nowhere to go but into his system—somewhere, everywhere—and it boiled angrily.

He was agitated, pulling at his bedclothes, ripping at the catheter, recognizing no one . . . or so we thought.

"Do you know who I am?" my mother asked him calmly one afternoon in the final days, prepared for a shrug and dreading the very thought.

His answer was quick.

"You are my precious, beautiful wife."

It was a fleeting moment, nothing more, but a treasure she will keep in her own special place forever. And then he was gone again.

If he ever saw another clown, or a man in gray with a child, or whether he put a face to the shadow, we never knew.

On the morning of October 12, a nurse checked and found no pulse. He was still breathing but raggedly.

"It won't be long now," the nurse told my mother. "He's going to die as he lived—with great dignity."

Four hours later, my mother left his side for just a moment. She would be right back, she said. Chuck's daughter, Jackie, the mother of the three little girls, was alone in the room, holding his hand, watching his chest slowly rise and fall. The dream catcher her girls had bought him lay by his side.

"Someone come!" Jackie called urgently.

And he was gone. Though he had been comatose for hours, somehow he still had the presence of mind to wait until his bride of more than half a century was out of the room, not wanting her to see him die. And as long as I am writing the unofficial history of this man's final times, it will remain thus. Let someone else call it simple coincidence. Nothing—*nothing*—was ever simple with them.

Fifty years after the transfusion of bad blood, twenty months after doctors said he was dying of liver disease, eighteen weeks after Hospice moved in to a terminal situation, sixteen days after all medication and food was removed, fourteen days after the first shadows appeared, two hours after the legendary basketball star Wilt Chamberlain died a coast away (and thus stole all the front-page headlines), Dad gave up.

The phone call to Atlanta came early that morning. Not much time, my mother said, her voice weary and full of pain; please come. I thought of all the other similar warnings but decided to heed this one, nonetheless, and began the long drive. In thick, five-lane, lunch-hour traffic just outside Charlotte, the car phone rang. He had been gone ten minutes. It was over.

I was in the outside lane and, stupidly, instead of trying to maneuver my way to the other side, I simply cried in my own little seventy-mile-an-hour world. From Charlotte to Greensboro, I believe, though I remember little of it. For all the expectations, there is nothing so sudden and startling as the moment it happens.

We stopped for a few minutes along the way and I sat on the hood of the car, alone, breathing in the pure fact of his death. It was not dark and threatening, as I had imagined this day to be. Instead, it was crystal clear and crisp. We had a chat, he and I, the first of hundreds to come over the next few months. The image in my mind was strong and virtual. He had only been dead for an hour or so and I was picturing the transition. If what he had been dreaming these last fifteen months—and indeed what he had been living these last seventy-eight years—was true, he was likely standing at the gate, in line, waiting to be processed. A thousand, no, a million spirits in front and behind. Some friends even.

Perhaps the process was instantaneous and he was already in the arms of his long-gone loved ones, the joy overwhelming. But what if the others were right and he was in purgatory, a kind of boot camp to determine his self-wealth? Or what if . . . ?

"You know what I'm hoping?" I said to the sky. "I'm hoping you're not disappointed right now."

There was the usual conglomeration of emotions attached. Anger, bitterness, a tremendous sense of emptiness. Why would I possibly be angry at my father for dying? As we always said to each other, the alternatives sure were more appealing. He surely didn't want to die, but for years I had silently, selfishly, wondered if he was doing enough to make sure he lived. A terrible accusation, certainly, and if the doctor and pharmacy bills were any indication, it seemed he was. Just to look at those calendars should be proof positive. And yet . . .

In that very first *Sporting Life* show in the spring of 1992, we also profiled a wonderful older man named Crash Davis. Yes, *that* Crash Davis of *Bull Durham* fame . . . the model for Kevin Costner's character. A former major-league shortstop who spent most of his seasons in the minors, and now here he was, all of seventy-six, still flirting with the girls, taking daily aerobics classes (the only man in the room, no less) . . . a robust man who loved life.

"I'm gonna live forever." He winked at me before launching Costner's memorable monologue from the film about "sweet, slow kisses" as he looked deeply into the eyes of the much-younger woman he was dating at the time.

Almost before I got back to the office from that shoot, I called Dad and told him about this great character, raved on about what great shape he was in—and gee whiz, "He's five years older than you, Dad!"

Five months later on the show, we told the story of Gene Shirk, at ninety-two still actively coaching the men's cross-country team at Albright College in Reading, Pennsylvania. Not a thing wrong with him; he was in his eighth decade of coaching. Married to a much-younger woman, obviously the absolute love of his life, he radiated health and happiness. He died two years later only because a tree got in the way of his car.

"Dad, you wouldn't believe this guy. Ninety-two! And still taking bus trips with his team, still up at the crack of dawn and running practices. Man, he's something."

Dad seemed to ignore my not-so-subtleties and gave me his best "can't wait to see that story" as he always did.

Over the years they came one after another, testaments to vigor and good health. And one by one, Dad admired them from afar. Opal

Trotter, the softball pitching great-grandmother from Springfield, Missouri. Carl Rhoer, the eighty-year-old hockey player from Iowa. Gene Sarazan, the ninety-four-year-old golfing legend. Hugh Alexander, the ageless scout for the Chicago Cubs. Max Patkin, still the baseball clown at seventy-seven. Red Klotz, the seventy-two-year-old basketball player-coach whose team played foil to the Harlem Globetrotters. Harry Caray, still doing the Cubs broadcasts well into his seventies.

While they were wonderful stories, to a man and woman, they also became my occasional unspoken redress to my father. See what you could be like, if only . . . ? Of course he couldn't. He was just a man with a bad back, carpal tunnel syndrome, a bad prostate, and a liver silently collapsing. But I had wanted him to be Hopalong Cassidy when I was little and I suppose I wanted him to be someone else when I was grown too.

Someone who would live forever.

In the small, dark hours of a Saturday morning four days later, as a vase of ashes sat ready to be entombed on one side of the United States, a thundering tremor rippled across the other side of the country. It began in the California desert but was felt as far away as Las Vegas, measuring 7.0 on the Richter scale.

"It didn't hurt much," said one casino employee to a television crew hours later, "just kinda scary, the way the chandeliers all shook."

Because the epicenter of the earthquake was underneath a tiny mining town called Hector, it became known for all time as the Hector earthquake.

Hector. As in USS *Hector*, my dad's ship during the war.

I have always believed in irony, that life is never simply happenstance. Everything occurs for a reason, with a purpose. And the months leading up to my father's death, and those that followed it, simply cemented that theory for me.

The evening of his burial, we gathered at my mother's apartment to sort out our emotions. It had been a long and tortured day, full of profound sadness. It was left to each of us, individually, to deal with this in our own way, to reach deep inside and examine how we felt and where we would go from this point. But collectively, we circled the wagons and put on brave smiles.

As we walked from the apartment into the night, leaving my mother there all alone for the first time in her life, a strange light came from overhead.

One by one, mouths agape, we looked up into the belly of the Goodyear blimp. It hovered directly over the complex, like a beacon in the starlit night. Where had it come from? Where was it going? Nothing was in town that we knew of that would attract it. And why would it choose this single complex over which to float, noiselessly, eerily?

We looked at each other in astonishment. I felt the floodgates begin to open once more and I could watch it no longer. The day began with a faraway earthquake and ended with a visit from on high. What would tomorrow bring? All we knew was, it would come without him.

Or would it?

chapter eighteen

the rookie class

■ OCTOBER 25, 1999

Two weeks after my father's death I was back in the office on a Monday morning, trying to get my life back in order, when a producer stuck his head in my door.

"The Pentagon just called our D.C. bureau," he said breathlessly. "There's a private jet out of control apparently, and they say Payne Stewart is on it."

Translation: quick obituary and then prepare to handle whatever comes.

"Who else is with him?" I asked quickly, my voice quivering.

"I don't know. But they say there are three or four other people on it."

My mind raced. Stewart was headed to Texas to do a site search for a course he was planning to design, and then traveling on to Houston for the season-ending tour championship. Were the other three or four passengers golfers? So many of them lived in one huge Orlando enclave. How big a disaster might this be? It would be big enough if it was only Stewart.

I sat stunned. I had become acquainted with the reigning U.S. Open golf champion over the years, had even spent a day the summer before at his house. We toured his closet together, me seeing for the first time the hundreds and hundreds of shirts and knickers that had become his trademark on tour. The closet was bigger than some apartments, with three large picture windows and a huge island in the middle. He was about to embark on what he called an "eleven-outfit trip"; eleven tournament days that demanded eleven different ensembles. I was having a tough time with the complicated baggage end of it, let alone accessorizing.

He laughed at my astonishment. "Help me lay them out here on this table."

There were dozens of shades of every color in the rainbow, mixtures of plaids and checks and outrageous patterns.

"Here," he said, "whaddya think goes with this?"

He laid a yellow shirt on the table and then turned to the bottom rack of knickers. Once we matched them up, he took me around the corner into another small room where a chest of drawers covered one entire wall, full of nothing but socks; each drawer with a different color or pattern. The shoes, hundreds of them in every possible style and color, were in another room in the basement, but to get to them you had to traverse a built-in putting green that ran from wall to wall to wall. Undulations here and there made pin positions tough and he used the green daily to hone his putting skills. It was precisely the kind of mansion you would expect of a young man who had made his fortune winning golf tournaments and endorsing everything from clothing to equipment. But this was in the days before his final Open championship. The house was on the market. He had no endorsement contracts to speak of. Life was good only because of his faith, for his business and golf life were suffering a bit. Still, he had the image to uphold and worked it like a science.

"How in the world do you pack? You must have to take five suitcases."

"Aw, I have it down pat. I take one large suitcase, one hanging bag, one shoe bag, and my golf bag. Course, you gotta remember, I rarely fly commercial so I don't usually have to hang around waiting or worry about the airlines losing anything."

Like so many of the young men on the golf tour, he usually leased a jet to travel from one tournament to the next. It was a fairly new "time share" idea, where they purchase as many hours as they figure they'll need for the year and the plane is always waiting, wherever they might need it. Occasionally they shared a ride, three or four golfers off to the same destination. Scott Hoch, a tour veteran and a close neighbor of Stewart's in Orlando, figured traveling this way had saved him twenty-nine days at home the previous year, nearly a month that would otherwise have been spent in hotels and airline terminals away from his family. And there was no way to measure that value—unless you don't make it home.

My day at Payne's home was one I will never forget and one that dwelled near the edge of my thoughts that Monday as I sat and worried. I even filled some time trying to imagine what was in the luggage at the rear of the small jet. Red plaid? Muted brown? And what was boiling within this remarkable young man as the ghost plane mysteriously charted its course for a South Dakota farmyard? He had changed so much over the years, from a brash kid in strange clothes to a warm and sensitive, religious man . . . in strange clothes. Somehow the clothes made sense in his latter years. And now he was about to die . . . if he hadn't already.

I made it through that day, making the rounds of our network shows, telling his tale as best I could. It wasn't easy, but we rolled out the footage of my tour of his closet and we talked of the private-jet arrangements and we argued the merits of being in the air as much as these men were, week after week.

But it was difficult for another reason for me. The emotions of having lost a father were still raw and spilling over into this new adventure with death. The only relief, one very much revolving around golf, was the discovery that no other player had been sharing Payne's ride this time. On the other hand, his agent and manager had been on board and their deaths affected not only golf but nearly every other sport, for they had many other athletes and coaches in their stable. It was one of the most devastating tragedies in sports history.

I flew to Houston for the tour championship, Payne's original destination, the next day to begin documenting the most somber and maudlin golf tournament in history. Nobody knew the pain within me still and I wasn't telling. It made no sense to burden them with my grief. They had their own to handle.

On a fog-bound Thursday dawn, they held a small service at the first tee at the Champions Club. A bagpiper's haunting melody came from down the fairway, and through that dense vapor, he slowly appeared as if a ghost. First his head and the pipes, then his body, an eerie sight at the best of times—and these were not. The best golfers in the world, so tough and impervious, sat soaked in tears, and I was no different, mine simply a spillover from the previous weeks but at least private. Tom Lehman, as good and decent a man as there is on the men's golf tour, somehow found the right words to say to all of us that morning. He talked of the great loss, of not being too proud to cry, of Payne being in a far better place now. It was over quickly, the fog enveloping the piper as he played his way back down that first fairway.

I was just one of dozens there that morning: paying tribute, absorbing the mist, and recycling it into tears. Everyone, if he bothered to notice, just assumed the tears were for Payne. And while they were, they had to be shared.

A day later, however, at the large memorial service back at Payne's hometown of Orlando, Florida, they became public.

I probably shouldn't have gone, shouldn't have forced myself to face such a traumatic situation again so soon. But I was there, wired up and live, as the network brought the world the two-hour service. When it was over, a voice in my ear informed me I was on camera. Another anchor wrapped up the service and turned to me.

"Jim, what are your thoughts as we bring this to a close?"

I meandered through some inane babble, when on the edge of subconscious a thought arose. And you would think, after years of experience, I would have learned to ignore such impulses until further, private examination. But I didn't.

"Leon, the thought keeps coming back to me. That there is a pretty strong rookie class of angels up there now. Wilt Chamberlain . . . Payne . . ."

And on international television, my voice drowned in a quick but very recognizable sob.

" . . . and my father."

When the lights were off and the man in my ear mumbled we were clear, I stripped off the wires and went to find a quiet corner. I was embarrassed, not because of my tears or my emotions, but for allowing them to intrude on my job. What had become of me? Once upon a time, I had been able to control such moments. Not now. But then, I had never lost my father and a good friend within days of each other.

I flew back to Houston alone that night to finish the tournament coverage, wallowing in my own emotional pity. What a fool I'd made of myself. Why had I done that? I'd been taught early in my career to avoid becoming part of the story at all costs; that the audience didn't care about me. I remembered once in my formative newspaper years, writing a column about how difficult it was getting an interview with a certain coach.

"Nobody cares how much trouble you have," my editor yelled at me correctly. "They only care if you got the quotes or not. It's nobody's business how tough your job is . . . nobody's business but yours."

And suddenly, in the gasp of a painful moment, I had not only broken the cardinal rule, but had held myself up for ridicule. *They're probably laughing at me—either that or preparing my walking papers,* I thought to myself.

But oddly enough the world—at least that world in the Houston press tent—seemed to understand. Many of my media colleagues hadn't gone to Orlando and so paid their respects through our television coverage.

"I didn't know about your father," they said almost in unison upon my return.

"I feel so . . . . stupid, so foolish," I mumbled to them.

"Don't!" they demanded. "You're human. We all felt what you felt. It's just that our loss was just a friend. Yours was so much more."

And they hugged me.

Three days later, that rookie class became even stronger when the great football star Walter Payton died. Another friend gone.

And I cried again, in a private corner this time, alone, and this time a kind of peace rolled over me. For I could see my father there in line, credentials in hand, proud to be a part of such an assemblage, Wilt, Payne, and Walter nearby, all waiting to get in. It's doubtful that trio had time to dream of white shadows or pickup trucks, for their ends came fairly fast. But somehow I knew he would tell them his wonderful, curious tales. Wilt would laugh that deep rumble of his and wonder if the shadows were tall, and Walter would ask why he hadn't stiff-armed the clowns, and Payne would have wondered why the man in gray hadn't had a more colorful wardrobe.

And all would be right.

Whether they all got past the gates of heaven is not for me to decide. I only know, deep in my soul, that my father's life—and more specifically, his faith—ushered him into the presence of God.

The ensuing months after his death took on vivid colors, etched in sharp contrasts. Everything that happened, it seemed, was connected to his passing, as if by an invisible string. Tragedy and death seemed to step forward, as if to offer startling perspective to what I was going through. Never more so than one out-of-the-blue assignment that came down from on high just six weeks after Dad died. CNN was preparing for its thunderous Millennium project, an entire weekend of special programming designed to look back at the twentieth century and to look ahead to the twenty-first.

It was rare that the news division of the network ever came to me with a request, except when they needed an athletic obituary or an overview of something from the sports world. They had requested an essay immediately following the Olympic Park bombing in 1996, and the ensuing few minutes, written in about a half hour, were the contribution that won the Emmy. But they usually left me to the whims of the sports department . . . until the world was about to turn A.D. 2000. After death, anno Domini—how appropriate.

"They want you to do a piece," said the news producer who would help me put it together, "on miracles. How, though the world has become increasingly mired in technology, it has continued to believe in God and His miracles."

Why they came to me and not another writer, I never asked. Once, years before, they had asked me to try out for the role of host on a new weekly series that dealt with the future. I enjoyed it; the producers felt I was right for it. But when it was presented to Ted Turner in what was then his monthly program reviews, he reportedly told them I was "too sports" to do such a different show. I was too readily identified with sports to make the crossover. That was a fence I had run into throughout my career. When the Gulf War droned on and the network needed replacement troops for the weary reporters stuck in the region, I rapidly volunteered. It was another experiment in relative importance. Why report on football and baseball when there are men and women being killed? Who cares about hockey when a war is going on? But again, I was "too sports," although toward the end of the war, there was talk of sending me to Jerusalem to report, much to my family's horror. The war ended, however, while that move was still in the talking stage.

Now came the strange request to depart from my usual sporting arena and take on such a wide and theological subject as miracles. I didn't think they knew at all of my father's fresh death but the coincidence couldn't have been better timed. Though I wasn't sure what form this commentary would take, I was still mired in grief enough to believe it was simply meant to be. And so I dived into one of the most fascinating and inspirational projects of my career, an investigation of miracles. Since they had given me no boundaries, I was free to shape and mold as I saw fit. I had begged for a miracle as recently as two months before, knowing full well that none was appropriate or available. And I wasn't certain I believed in them anyway. But in researching the subject, I began to change my mind.

I learned the story of Audrey Santo, the teenager from near Boston who had become what is called the "Apostolate of the Silent Soul." She had fallen in the family swimming pool when she was little, lost a great deal of oxygen to the brain, and thus suffered massive hypoxia. She had lived, but in a strange, eyes-open coma, gradually performing what believers near and far came to call miracles. Just being in her presence, apparently, was enough to make the disabled walk and the blind see again. Odd substances flowed from the myriad of religious icons that lined the walls of the converted garage. Whether she subconsciously, through her "silent soul," performed miracles was not for me to declare, simply report.

Audrey and Padre Pio and Father Chaminade, sightings of the Virgin Mary at Fatima, Lourdes, and Medjugorje, all led me closer to the confirmation of an old hunch that some things are beyond most of our control. From Boston to France to Yugoslavia and a farm in Wisconsin, miracles apparently occur. Ask the Plains Indians about hunches. When a rare white buffalo was born on the Heiders' farm on the banks of the Rock River a few years ago, it was immediately called "Miracle" because, to Native Americans across the land, it was a messenger of creation, an important sign of well-being, and they continue to make pilgrimages to pray at the huge animal's side. A one-in-six-billion birth to us, a miracle to them. A hunch? Hardly.

It obviously is not simply a hunch for the Vatican, either, which has long had a council known by several names but commonly called "the miracle police." A gathering of doctors, scientists, theologians, and Vatican officials investigates the countless tales of "miracles" to determine their authenticity and subsequent canonization of those who perform them, leading to sainthood. Since it takes a confirmed miracle to complete the final phase for beatification, they must be true, at least in the eyes of the Roman Catholic Church.

Where was the miracle when my father needed one? Such a question surely never even crossed his mind and would likely have had me banished from the corridors of the pure. But just like dealing with the Payne Stewart tragedy, researching and then writing the "Miracle" essay just a few weeks after Dad's death allowed me another crutch as I hobbled toward some kind of acceptance of our loss.

chapter nineteen

father's day evidence

My mother was the rock among us all. As we wondered how long it would be before she could possibly go back to stay alone in their apartment, she shocked us all by returning there the very night of his death. The first full night of sleep she had enjoyed in months.

"Sooner or later," she said, "I'll have to do it . . . so why not sooner?"

We still walked on eggshells, not wanting to disturb her fragile balance, for we knew she was on the edge, teetering. But at every turn, she widened our eyes. While I broke down at the slightest prompt and my brother wandered about tearless, unable to let anything flow, she began the rest of her life. It's not that she didn't mourn—she will the rest of her life—and it's not that she didn't occasionally double over with the pain of her loss; it is simply she saw little use in curling up in some corner. If she longed to join him, she kept that to herself.

Dad's memorial service was held several weeks after his death, to allow friends and family to gather from long distances. As we planned the simple ceremony at their Methodist church, Mom declared that she was going to speak.

"You're kidding," I immediately stammered. "You think that's wise?"

"You know," she said, "I watched Payne Stewart's memorial and I saw his wife get up so bravely and talk about their life together and how much he had meant to her. And I said to myself right then, 'I can do that.' If she can do it, so can I."

And so she did. Bolstered by a nearby pew, she valiantly stood before the astonished crowd and had her say. Friends from the church and community sat near the front. Dad's brother and his wife, his little sister and her husband, had driven in from Pennsylvania. A flock of Girl Scouts sat in awed confusion near the back. They had come often as a group to the complex where my parents lived, to sing and dance and, in the long run, be entertained. They seemed to love my father, hovered around him, endured his teasing. He was often the only man among the dozens of women there. And what they were watching this particular afternoon must have been both puzzling and inspiring. They were saying good-bye to an old friend, some perhaps for the first time in their young lives, and watching that old friend's wife gather courage from somewhere deep inside and stand in front to talk. Chances are, if only one of them remembers that moment somewhere down her own line, she will be all the better for it.

Firm and loving, never once did my mother lose her way. It was as it always had been, after all.

"This is a remembrance; it's not a funeral," she said. "We are here to remember the pleasant things, and for me, that begins when I was six years old and he was nine. We met in Sunday school and I thought he was pretty cute."

The gathering chuckled at the thought. It was the perfect lift to what could have been a maudlin few minutes and she seemed to gain strength from her own lightness.

"From that young age, I admired him. We were married nearly fifty-eight years. Next month would have been fifty-eight—almost a lifetime together. And he left a wonderful legacy to me . . . to all of us. Two wonderful sons, four wonderful grandchildren, three great-grandchildren."

Those final words took so much out of her that anything else she had planned to say would have to wait for another time. She took a painful breath, smiled bravely, and sat down.

Slowly, when she had finished, I made my way to the pulpit, where she had wanted me to stand for so very long. I took a deep breath, looked over at my mother and then out at the congregation.

"You know, in my business, they say you should never follow children or animal acts," I began, "but may I now add mothers to that list?"

I told them of my plans for this book and read them a small excerpt from my earliest draft, just a few chosen words about his dreams of heaven and where he figured he was going. I made it perhaps halfway through before a catch in my breath stopped me. Who would have figured the professional talker in the family would have the toughest time? My brother, who is a paid soloist at a prominent D.C. church, sang "The Lord's Prayer," never once giving hint that he was singing for a father gone just days. It was I among the threesome left clutching at my soul—at least publicly. We all were, deep inside.

Back at her apartment, Mom remained the bravest of us.

"Um," we approached cautiously, not knowing what her reaction would be, "sooner or later, you're going to have to clean out his clothes. Whenever you're ready—and take your time, for sure—we'll be here to help."

"Well"—she looked up with a pained smile—"why not now?"

And with that, she put aside what she was doing and walked back to the bedroom. In an hour, almost all of his clothes were packed and ready to be parceled out here and there.

"You want all these," she said to me, not a question but a statement. There seemed no doubt in her mind. She had a couple of decades' worth of Father's Day gifts spread out on the bed.

For as long as I had covered professional golf—and if I had one television beat, as such, it was that—I reported each year from the major championships, the Masters, the U.S. and British Opens, and the PGA Championship. The United States Open invariably falls on Father's Day weekend and so always made for a very easy gift. Every year, as soon as I checked in on Monday and got my credentials, I headed to the merchandise tent and found something I thought he would enjoy: a shirt, a wind shirt, a jacket, all with the Open logos on the left breast. It was mailed that day and he knew to expect his present midweek. For years and years, that was our ritual and he would proudly wear whatever I sent to church that next Sunday morning, the first in his group to have the latest Open logo, wearing it before the final round had even been played.

"Oh, thanks for the shirt; it's great," he would say when I called from the course. "I wore it to church this morning and all the guys were so jealous."

There, on the bed, were the symbols of golfing Valhallas . . . Shinnecock Hills, Olympic Club, Oakmont, Pebble Beach, Pinehurst, Congressional, like a clothing Hall of Fame. I had to turn away, for I could still see his chest beating so joyfully inside them.

"You do want them, don't you?" she asked this time.

"No, Mom, I couldn't do that. You find someone else. Surely there are a lotta folks who would love these. I just, well . . ."

"I understand."

On the Monday before the 2000 U.S. Open, nine months after his death, I passed by the huge merchandise tent at Pebble Beach and could not summon the courage to enter. Sadly, it was on my route from the media center to the eighteenth green where we did post-round interviews and so I passed it hourly. An enormous cavern filled with thousands of golf shirts, jackets, sweaters, hats, everything and anything a souvenir-hunting fan could ask for. I would have certainly found another wind shirt for him, a pullover or a Hogan cap. In fact there was, in that pile of gifts on her bed, a frayed golf shirt from the 1992 Open held at that same venue. The circle was complete.

And now, years later when Father's Day morning came again, I slipped out the front door of the house we had rented along Seventeen-Mile Drive, ambled through the woods and across the fairways, and found my way to the beach. The sky was gray and ominous, the Pacific surf pounding against the huge rocks. I climbed to the top of one of them and sat for a while, my head in my hands, my heart in my throat. I was lost. I had no father to buy for, no father to call, no father to watch my work, no father to hug. After so many years of diffidence, only to finally come to terms with him as a man and a father, he was gone. It was Father's Day and he was gone.

I wondered if perhaps, in retrospect, I should have taken a few of those old gifts, as reminders. As if I needed anything tangible.

Oddly enough, much of his closet came from me. In the days when I was anchoring every night, with a wardrobe full of suits, he would not allow me to get rid of any of them. He didn't like to shop and, in truth, couldn't afford to. And so whenever I was finished with a suit or sports coat or tie, he would take the hand-me-down and wear it like it was brand new. I always felt strange about it but whatever pride welled up in his chest, he felt, was covered with good material. I often took him shopping, but in the end, he seemed to prefer what I'd passed along.

At his granddaughter's wedding, a month before he died, he wore a twenty-year-old suit of mine and a tie I had bought for him in the Bahamas during the LBJ administration.

"You look so spiffy," they all raved. And he did.

As she went through the drawers of Dad's chest next to his bed, she came across his old, worn wallet. There was his driver's license with two years left to go before expiration. Robert William Huber. Born: 11-1-20. Height: 6 feet. Weight: 180. Gray hair, brown eyes. There was a Civil Service I.D. card, an insurance card, a card from the Veterans Administration authorizing his hospitalization if necessary. A Social Security card, one of the very first meted out in 1938. A Sears and Roebuck credit card, the only one he allowed himself. (They had done business with Sears for nearly sixty years.) There was a tiny slip of paper with the heading "Complaint Form" and underneath, "State the nature of complaint below." A box no larger than a quarter-inch square sat ready for whatever lengthy complaint was necessary. My father's sense of humor.

And hidden away, folded neatly, was a ten-dollar bill.

"He probably had forgotten it was there," my mother says with a laugh today. "He always had trouble keeping money. He never knew how much he had so he'd tuck away a few dollars for emergencies.

"He'd ask if I wanted to go out and get something to eat and I'd ask him if he had any money. 'You need money?' I'd kid him. And he'd just say, 'Oh, I don't know.'

"Every once in a while, we'd be out shopping and I'd see something I liked and he'd dig into that old wallet and pull out some of his saved money and buy it for me as a surprise. For as much trouble as we had with finances, he always seemed to save something, even if it was a dollar."

In their tiny second bedroom sat boxes full of the paraphernalia of his crafts. Hundreds of feet of thin wire that was to be transformed into miniature trees, glued eventually to craggy rocks sparkling with minerals. Squint and you could imagine the wind-blown, sun-splashed coast of California. He turned them out by the dozens, selling them in craft shows or giving them to friends and family. They were, in effect, metal bonsai trees and people loved them.

Strangely, however, in the end, he simply forgot how to make them.

"He would sit and look at that wire for the longest time," my mother recalled, "and have no earthly idea what to do with it. Something he'd done with such ease for so many years, just gone."

And where? He did not become the least bit senile in his dying months, the edge to his humor still remarkable, the big brown eyes still alive with an intelligence and warmth that makes one wonder if he didn't merely, and subconsciously, replace that bit of knowledge with something far more important to his journey. There is, after all, only so much room.

My mother, Methodist at this stop in her life, could never mask the Presbyterian nature in her.

"What's meant to be will be," she would say with great authority.

And so she merely chuckled when the network announced that *The Sporting Life* would return, at long last after a year away, and weekly now. She never said but I'm sure she was thinking that the good Lord gave me time enough off to handle Dad's dying and then gave me the show back for a while, for balance.

I thought about that often as I stood on a warm January day amid the devastation along the Venezuelan mountainside, working on our very first story back on the show. Major-league baseball players who were born and raised there were returning to try to raise money to help, and I was along to document their efforts.

"Do you know where we are?" our driver said in passable English. The four-wheel drive was slowly, tediously maneuvering over a horrible dirt road. The storm that had unleashed the furious mudslides on a terrifying morning five weeks earlier had devastated miles and miles of houses and property. They were estimating 100,000 people dead, some buried in their cars, most in their homes. They may never officially know the final death toll.

"It's just a road," I answered, looking around at the huge rocks. "And not much of one."

"No. Look closely," he said. "We're driving over a three-story building."

We stopped and got out. Sure enough, you could see the roof tiles occasionally sticking out of the ground. Trucks full of families passed us slowly, on their way for the first time since the slides to see what was left of their homes, their lives.

You could smell the death beneath us. A Portuguese man and his family had come here half a century before to open the grocery store that was now just a rooftop. If they had escaped, no one knew. The wheels of a baby carriage protruded from the cementlike mud. Was there a child's body inside? Our driver's home was a block away, untouched. The river of mud and boulders had mysteriously just stopped a hundred feet from his door. Neighbors, best friends, were gone.

He crossed himself and raised his hands in resignation.

I walked aimlessly, my cameraman busy shooting elsewhere. I kicked at the rocks and ran my hand along the ankle-high streetlight and began to feel an emotional riptide. I looked up and felt Dad's presence and just shook my head.

"Believe this?" I whispered. "Isn't this the worst thing you've ever seen? Wasn't there anything that could've been done?"

As though he had somehow taken charge in just three months.

The tears that were on the edge never came. The lump in my throat subsided. Is this what you've prepared me for, Dad? Did I have to go through your death to understand life? Am I better prepared now?

Are there no more tears left?

"Where you're standing," came a voice, "was a church."

Startled out of my reverie, I turned to our driver who had apparently been there for a while.

"A church? Right here?" I asked.

"Yes. Look, there, see the cross? That was on the steeple."

He looked at me curiously, seeing deep inside me.

"You, you're not handling this well, eh?"

"No," I answered, "but how could anyone handle this well?"

"Have you had anyone die near you?"

"My father, just recently."

"Ah."

And he turned and, without another word, walked slowly back to the car. I followed, curious.

"And you, Alvaro? How about you?"

He looked off into the rubble. They had discovered one boulder weighing at least ten tons that had been swept off the top of the mountain, carried in the fury of the raging mud through home after home. One ten-ton boulder, multiplied by a thousand score. Imagine.

"Me?" he slowly answered. "How can I count? Maybe thousands. We were a close community, friends, family. All gone."

His young eyes, dark like coal, glistened and he turned away. I had lost one and had trouble finding the justice, the equity. He had lost a fair-sized city and yet there was a common thread. Though we never talked of it again and I would leave two days later, probably never to see him again, we would share man's grief forever.

The irony will never end, it seems.

"Derrick Thomas just died," came my marching orders. "Huberize it. You spent some time with him, didn't you? We'll pull the video."

The great Kansas City Chiefs linebacker had been partially

paralyzed in a snowy accident just weeks before but had appeared to be improving. Doctors even said his condition was far better than they first thought. Would he walk again? The miracles are only just beginning at the spinal-cord center in Miami, the site of several *Sporting Life* stories over the years. It was where dreams were harbored.

And then the thirty-three-year-old athlete simply clutched his chest and died of a massive stroke.

As I hunched over the keyboard, preparing yet another obituary, my mind drifted back seven years. I had never met Thomas until then but knew his reputation was among the most remarkable in all of sports. A tireless worker in the community, he had begun a literacy program for inner-city children, and every Saturday that the Chiefs were home during the fall, he would gather them at a library and read to them. He was the NFL's Humanitarian of the Year only once but could have retired the trophy if they'd stretched the rules. And now, as I caught up with him that day in 1993, he was about to give the keynote address at the Veterans Day gathering before the Vietnam Memorial.

His father, a captain in the air force, had been shot down in the jungles of Vietnam when Derrick was just five. They officially declared his father dead seven years later, having never found his body. But in the young son's mind and heart, he would never die.

"I hardly knew him and yet I knew every single thing about him, more than I know about anybody else in my life," Thomas told me. "He taught me so much, even in death, about how to live. Whenever I came to a fork in the road, he always seemed to be there to give me the right directions. I can't quite explain that but, well, you know . . ."

I didn't at the time . . . but I was learning.

chapter twenty

a chat with an angel

■ JULY 2000

It was rare that I ever consulted my father when I made career changes. He seemed content in the past tense, thoroughly intrigued by the process and anxious to know how it would go. I would tell him that an offer had been made, a chance was apparent, but I rarely asked his opinion, for he had never been a part of the industry and knew little of its workings.

But on a cool, gray day in early July beside one of Wimbledon's back courts, as two unknown Europeans played an opening-round match to a gallery of one (or two), I asked what he thought about my latest challenge. I had done some work over the years for the other elbows of Turner Broadcasting's enormous collection of networks but always on a freelance basis, maintaining my steady base with CNN. Before I ever enlisted with that operation, while I was still with the NBC affiliate in Atlanta, I wrote a six-hour documentary on a year in the life of the Atlanta Braves baseball team called "A Long Way to October" and that had opened doors that remained ajar for more than two decades. I hosted the PGA Championship and the Grand Slam, did features and essays for the Goodwill Games and the Winter Olympics and a few other TBS and TNT events. I even managed to appear several times on Cartoon Network, which must always be one of the most glaring inclusions on any live person's résumé. (To rub shoulders, as it were, with Scooby Doo and Wile E. Coyote is a rare treat, don't you think?) I had talked often about coming on board Turner Sports full-time but there were never enough events to warrant such a move. As I was working their coverage of Wimbledon in the summer of 2000, word came that the time was now right.

They had added a half-season of NASCAR events to three major golf championships, figure skating, Wimbledon, Goodwill Games and, of course, coverage of the NBA three nights weekly. More than enough now to keep an essayist and commentator in search of words.

And so I sat in the vacant bleachers on court 15 that day at Wimbledon and broached the subject to my father.

"Pretty good deal," I said to the sky. "Whaddya think?"

I don't know what I was expecting but there was no whisper, no rustle of the wind, no tap on my shoulder. I looked around to see whether anyone was watching me talk to . . . myself.

"I've been with CNN sixteen years," I continued under my breath. "Should I give that up?"

I was in the midst of a summer-long journey that most sports fans would have given their right arm to take. I had stood beside Tiger Woods at Pebble Beach in June as he accepted the U.S. Open championship trophy after breaking every imaginable record. I went from California directly to London to work Wimbledon where I would witness the Williams sisters make tennis history, where Pete Sampras would break the grand-slam record. From London, I would drive north (on the wrong side of the road and the wrong side of the car, a combination that was nearly lethal any number of times) to St. Andrews in Scotland where I would once again chronicle the marvels of Mr. Woods as he continued his golfing onslaught. There, in the shadows of the game's creators, he would become the youngest career winner of the grand slam in history and we would stand shoulder-to-shoulder in its aftermath. I would return home for a brief rest before going on to Louisville, Kentucky, where Tiger would win the PGA Championship. And we would finish our historic summer together in Toronto as he won the Canadian Open two weeks later.

It was a three-month odyssey that will surely remain among my fondest memories for the rest of my life. Tiger and I had become friends of sorts, as close as athlete and announcer can get, and it was a relationship I enjoyed immensely. Dad and I often talked about this bright young man and how he would surely change the game, how fortunate I was to come along in the Tiger era, when I could explore his psyche to paint the portrait of a master at work. If I took the new job, I explained to the sky that day at Wimbledon, I would be able to continue on the periphery of such a monumental excursion, working a few golf tournaments a year. But I would be giving up the chance to be there on a weekly basis.

And I would have to give up *The Sporting Life* after nearly ten years. Very few in my industry have ever been so blessed, to be handed such a vehicle and allowed to do with it what they wanted. I don't believe that the decision makers who signed on to that show in 1991 thought it would take such an emotional highway. They wanted a storyteller to tell stories, plain and simple. But the storyteller wanted more. To give up two very satisfying challenges such as covering Tiger Woods and being the heart and soul of *The Sporting Life* was not an easy decision.

"You have a gift, my friend," said the old basketball Hall of

Famer Cazzie Russell near the end of a second *Sporting Life* story we did with him in the spring of 2000. I had discovered the former college All-American and New York Knicks star working as a high school assistant coach in Columbus, Ohio, giving back to the kids while he was working as the full-time minister of a downtown church. The president of a small midtown school in Georgia called Savannah College of Art and Design was in the process of trying to begin an athletic program and knew he would need a big-name coach to draw students. He saw our story, called Russell, and talked him into coming south.

When we went to Savannah four years later to revisit Cazzie, I asked him where he was going to go next.

"Oh, I doubt anywhere." He laughed in that big, thunderous voice of his. "I've got my own church, the job here at the school is great . . . where could I go? But then again, Mr. Huber"—and he drew the name out to seven syllables—"you seem to have a better pipeline upstairs than I do. You found me in Columbus; you got me here. Maybe *you* can tell *me* where I'm going next.

"You definitely seem to have a gift, my friend."

Would that gift be best put to use by staying or going? Could I put my pipeline to work elsewhere? I had worked myself into a position where it was now these kinds of questions that determined my career path. The days of the five-dollar-a-week raise being the only reason for moving, thankfully, were history.

Dad said nothing that day at Wimbledon I could hear. But he said things I could feel and I knew he approved. I had already made up my mind and I guess he knew that. But I somehow needed to let him know he was going to be in on the process from now on. I needed to move on. Who knew? *The Sporting Life* had been resurrected once, why not again? If you believe hard enough . . .

"C'mon," I said, nodding skyward, "let's go watch Sampras."

I didn't originally intend to put my father's dying days to paper. Such an idea, at the outset, would seem morally absurd. But as he gathered us at his feet each day, as children to the oracle, and told us of his passing, explained his trauma and joy, remembered his dreams and revisited his nightmares, I would immediately write them down afterward for fear of forgetting. It seemed terribly important then, as it still does today.

Each and every time I visited, at the beginning of the illness and at the end, he offered a memory that will last me the rest of my life. I look back at my notes, scribbled here and there, and I feel his presence at hand. And he knew full well what a powerful finish he was preparing. At last he would be successful at something. For all his life, he had wanted to be somebody, to do something important. He never knew who or how . . . until the end. It's not to say he went out bathed in drama and pathos, putting together his tales of dark angels and heavenly walks and awaiting that final curtain call. I truly believe he knew that, although everyone must die, he was being given a chance to die with dignity and humor and intelligence. And through him, we were all being given a tiny glimpse of what awaits.

There are those who will tell us that this man's fertile imagination began building a world as soon as he knew time was nigh. That his dreams were nothing more than subconscious wishes. Normal.

Because we are left with a choice in the matter, I prefer to find substance in those shadows, reality in the absurd. He believed in them, found both fear and solace and even a bit of humor in them. The dreams of a dying man provided a pathway for those struggling to comprehend what he was going through.

He was going to heaven, after all, in a pickup truck and didn't that seem perfectly normal?

What did my father's death teach me? What lessons did I learn from his passing? I wonder, even today. If he had died an agonizing, excruciating death, would it have been the same wonderful journey? If he had left abruptly, struck by a bus or the faulty valve, would I be spending this time examining the process? Probably not, but he didn't and wasn't. He was able to take us gently along with him, a stationary tour guide, allowing us to sit by his side, listen to his tales, and appreciate the adventure for what it was. If he had been an angry, bitter man, fighting the tug-of-war with hourly venom, would I see death any differently today? But he wasn't and didn't, and I do.

Do I fear death any less today because of what he taught me along his way? Probably so, for he never settled things within himself until the last half year or so, never accepted his fate until Hospice joined hands with him. I don't fear death as an abstract. I realize it's just the way we were designed; not for longevity or durability necessarily, but for achievement. Perhaps a day will come (probably about the end of time—and wouldn't that be appropriate?) when we will discover the secret to eternal life while we're on this planet. But until then, we have to accept our fate. And so I don't fear death as an abstract. But I still dread death immensely as a reality. I am full of apprehension. I like it here. I don't want to leave. I am bound by a thirsty sense of tomorrow.

They say an asteroid is headed toward Earth, to perhaps jolt us in about seventy-five years. I'd like to be around to see what happens. I want to be here when Tiger breaks all of Nicklaus's records. I want to know if the Braves will ever win another World Series. (And if I wonder that about the Braves, imagine the poor folks in Chicago and Boston.) I want to know if there will still be Social Security when my son is eligible. I wonder about global warming and how it will change our planet. Doctors say our baby girls will never have to worry about breast cancer; by the time our daughters are candidates, researchers will have found a cure.

I have a great curiosity about everything large and small. There is far too much left for me to accomplish and I fear having that taken away. And so from a personal standpoint, I learned that I'd just as soon put it off as long as possible.

I lost a loved one. I lost my father. People say, "You didn't *lose* anybody. He died. He didn't pass away. He died. The sooner you say the word, the healthier you'll become." And yet I *did* lose my father, at least his physical presence. And I fear losing others around me now that I have seen the tremendous void left. There comes a vacuum that can be filled only by the spirit. And that spirit, while a sturdy, viable companion, cannot help repair a light fixture, cannot explain how an engine works, cannot physically give me one more hug and tell me that he loves me. All he can do is be my conscience and that should be good enough . . . but it's not.

He remains, and that is enormously comforting. And yet he is gone, and that is still terribly disturbing.

My wife's father died while he was still young, barely fifty, but a victim of heart disease for years. And when my father-in-law suddenly was gone, she was devastated, torn asunder. He was her hero, her "Daddy," and he had treated her and her two sisters like princesses. There he had been, in a small house filled with women, and he had loved every second of it. Whether he could afford it or not (and he usually couldn't, but that hardly mattered), he would take them to the store and buy them new dresses . . . and drive their beaus those twenty-six miles back to college, if need be. He was the smiling, shining knight to his girls and they dearly, dearly loved him.

When he died, Carol seemed the hardest hit, though each of them fought with her own personal demons until she came to terms with his departure. It took Carol a few years and some deep therapy before she finally broke down and cried over his death, an agonizingly long and uncomfortable time hidden deep inside a fragile soul, but she turned quickly to my father for emotional sustenance.

"My daddy's gone now," she bravely told my father, the first time she saw him after her own dad's death, "and I won't ever have a daddy again. But I have a dad."

And she hugged him for all she was worth. I had yet to come to terms with him at that point, still saw him as distant and unemotional, and wondered at her reaction, wondered if this is the way someone handles the death of a loved one. There is no set of rules, no guide, no absolutes. She was simply following her own path and it was altogether right. I watched them hug, a tiny girl in a large man's arms, and envied her a bit. Not her loss, certainly, but her gain.

They remained close, beating me to his emotional doorsteps by years, until he left her too.

And she, too, has met him since his death.

The call came at work eight months after my father's death. "Jim," said a friend who had been with her, "they've taken Carol to the emergency room. I think she's had a heart attack. You'd better come quickly. She's so afraid she won't make it."

We spent eight hours that Friday in the ER, doctors desperately trying to figure out how her blood pressure had risen so furiously high, how her pulse rate managed to stay so torrid. It had happened to a slighter degree the weekend before, beckoning another, albeit shorter, emergency-room journey. They found little cause then and were just as baffled six days later. Cardiologists hovered, barked orders, gave prescriptions, made decisions, inserted tubes and belts and gadgets, and still knew very little.

The fear that settled into my bones that second Friday, resting my chin on my hands as I watched her cry, was staggering, breathtaking. We had gone through our share of ups and downs over the decades. Could I stand to lose her after all these years? Did I learn anything at all from my father's death? Was there a connection, a common thread? As she silently sobbed, scared witless, I glanced often at the heart monitor over her head as it kept track of her pressure. Doctors would come and go, nurses checking occasionally. There was little, it seemed, they could do.

Emergency rooms had been a thing of our collective youth. She had apparently inherited migraine headaches from her father and we seemed to make weekly excursions to the hospitals for help. They grew to know us by first name and had the proper medication waiting. At first, it was terrifying to me and I broke every speed law imaginable getting her to the hospital. She was in such unimaginable pain, something I had never seen or felt, and I thought she must surely be dying. Soon I learned to accept it, understand it, know that she would likely outgrow them, and she did. But this was different. Headaches weren't life threatening, I discovered; 220 over 110 was.

Finally, after hours and hours, the pulse leveled and the heart rate settled. She seemed out of the woods. They ordered a heart monitor and settled on medication.

It would be weeks of search and seizure, trying to find the cause. Everyone had an idea; no one had a clue. They knew that her heart was strong but whatever was driving it was furious. In the end, they hit upon a medicated answer and she stabilized and was better.

One night, weeks later, she awoke with a start. We were in Los Angeles where I was working a golf tournament. The bed was small, the room cramped, and sleep came in waves. She rarely traveled with me, preferring to separate work and play, but we had friends in L.A. and it seemed a good mix.

I was half asleep when she suddenly sat up in bed.

"What's wrong?" I asked. She took great delight, most mornings, telling me in gaudy detail of her latest dreams. They made such little sense to either of us that I usually hid in my morning newspaper and ignored her. This, however, seemed different.

"I just saw Dad," she said, referring to my father. Not "Daddy," for that was her name for her own father; just "Dad."

"Huh?"

"I was at the hospital, sitting with Mother and Daddy," she slowly remembered. "Your mother came out of a room, leading Dad by the hand. He held one arm out straight beside him, for some reason. I rushed over and hugged him and . . ."—she caught her breath, the scene so real it was staggering—"and he looked down at me as he always did, with that little smile on his face, and said, 'I'm so glad you're feeling better.' He knew. He knew I'd been so sick. It was just so, so real."

That her mother and father had been there was nothing new. She dreamed of them weekly, their presence almost reassuring to her. But I had been the only one to dream of Dad until that night.

"That's so good. Go back to sleep," I said. "Maybe you can catch up to him."

The difference between the way she handled her father's death and the way I handled mine was vast but simple. She had no preparation. The dinner simply went cold, and so did she, after the call came that night in 1967. I, on the other hand, had months to try to settle things, work all of this out in my head and in my heart before he died. It made it no easier and, in some ways, simply stretched out the emotional war within, but at least I managed to get all my questions out. Answers? Like waves to a beach, they slowly, steadily, come in. Some gently; some with great thunder.

As I continue to deal with it—and I suppose I shall forever, for he never will be too far from my consciousness—I will sort out more and more. We will never have all the answers but perhaps we shouldn't. It would make the questions meaningless, then.

But while I have cried a lot and felt his presence, sensed him around me often over the months, my brother has not. He, as Carol did with her father's death, has kept it deep inside. There have been no tears, though he probably feared he was dangerously close the morning that we went back into the sanctuary after everyone had left the service, picked up the vase with the ashes inside, and carried it, together, to the small space that my mother had purchased a few weeks before; so new that the plaque had yet to be screwed on. He took a deep breath, put his arm around my shoulders, and we stood there in silent prayer, having just buried our father. He trembled a bit, but not a tear came.

Six months later, I told him of my visitations, of the branches that scolded me, of the voice that had let me know I'd been caught. I asked Chuck how many times he'd felt the same way. Had Dad returned to him?

"No," was the answer, short and not so sweet. He said nothing else, that being enough. Whether he regretted the fact or felt I was storytelling again, I never learned. It was simply "no" and we moved on to another subject quickly.

My son, Matt, seems much the same as my brother. He had once lost a close friend to a car accident but had never been related to death when his "Poppa" died. What was going on deep inside him is anyone's guess, for he shows little emotion. Perhaps it is the stoic Native American in him. Part Cherokee, part Comanche, adopted at the tender age of six weeks, he was the light in his grandfather's eye. They had begun having serious discussions about who-knew-what almost before Matt learned to talk, sitting beside one another on a couch. Dad would read to him, Matt would try to return the favor, or they would simply study the ceiling.

As he grew into a young man, his grandfather took great pride in him, rode the great emotional teenage roller coaster with him, despaired at his turmoils, and rejoiced at his successes. He was never judgmental, leaving that to the young man's parents, and seemed to accept whatever life dealt. My parents always said that since I was the first to come along, they learned on me and perhaps that was one of the lessons, for they rolled evenly with every punch the entire family took.

When the illness began its march through my father's body, Matt tried to spend as much time as he could with him. They were both adults now but they would sit side by side once again, bringing back memories of long ago, giggling and telling stories. And we left them to their retreat, peeking around the corner occasionally, stifling a tear.

When the end came and Matt joined us for the funeral, he continued to show very little emotion. If he was upset, it seemed to be more for me than for him. But I know just as I lost a father, as my mother lost a husband and companion, he lost a great friend and it hurt deeply. Someday we will talk about it perhaps.

Or not.

Am I the only one to cry? And why?

We each handle death in our own individual way. Now that I've found my own niche, I've begun to notice others. In the initial hours of the twenty-first century, two young professional basketball players left the morning practice session, got into their sports cars, and roared out of the Charlotte parking lot. The speed limit on Tyvola Road is forty-five but they were twice that, maybe more, when David Wesley looked in his rearview mirror and saw his best friend spin and then crash. Wesley was on the phone with his fiancée.

"Call 911," he screamed at her, "and then call Kendall. Bobby's crashed behind me."

By the time Wesley had turned and made his way back to the crash scene, Bobby Phills was dead. Other players from the NBA team, on their way home, stopped in tragic astonishment. Their captain and the soul of their club was lying on the pavement, gone.

The paramedics were about to remove Phills's body from the scene when Kendall Phills drove up. His wife and the mother of their young son asked them to put him down.

"Give me five minutes with him," she said quietly, "just five minutes."

And with that, she knelt at her dead husband's side, took his lifeless hand, and talked to him.

"There were things left to be said," she remembers, "we were such close friends as well as husband and wife. I couldn't let them take him away without saying good-bye."

Wesley, meanwhile, and his teammates were in the middle of their season. Somehow, some way, they had to gather themselves and return to their jobs, playing a game for a living. And so they said their farewells on a hardwood court, muddling through the remaining games.

Wesley, who was charged with reckless driving, contended they hadn't been racing that morning but admitted the speed far exceeded the limit. Waves of guilt rolled over him as he tried to comprehend that moment and its consequences. He wore his friend's number 13 on his own uniform and his grief deep inside. It took him months to recover. When the team voted to turn his late friend's captaincy over to David, he finally took the number 13 off his jersey, let his grief subside, and became one of the best players in the NBA.

While Kendall Phills handled her husband's sudden death her way, David Wesley took another route. Neither is right, neither is wrong, for there is no rule book, I'm finding.

On a humid, dank August morning in Louisville, Kentucky, Jack Nicklaus was preparing to play in his final PGA Championship; the end of the most remarkable major championship career in golf history but also the end of one of the most emotional summers in Jack's life. He had made it clear that 2000 would be the final year he would play the four majors and so each stop became a ceremony, each move a photo op. If he wasn't caught sitting on a fence overlooking the Pacific Ocean at the U.S. Open, he was standing atop the bridge over St. Andrews' Swilken Burn in his final British Open. And now came the last stop.

The phone call he had been expecting, dreading, came early in the week. His mother, suffering for years, had finally died in Columbus, Ohio. Surely, Jack would withdraw from the championship and make his way home, the eldest son taking charge. He did go home for a day but returned to play the first two rounds of the PGA. His last two, as it would turn out, for he didn't make the cut.

"She always told me never to let her get in the way of any major championship," he told me, eyes still red and puffy after one of the saddest weeks of his life. He had come to join me in the TV tower overlooking the eighteenth green and we had to kick each other under the table to keep from breaking down. "She would have wanted me here. She was a tough old German and she lived a good, long life. My father was the one who was my golf coach, my mentor, my best friend, and she was the one who held the family together."

I had watched him play that final round on Friday alongside Tiger Woods, another symbolic torch passed between golfing giants, and I wondered what Tiger must have been thinking. He would occasionally sneak a peek at the old champion next to him and smile a little, knowing what Nicklaus was going through and probably wondering how he himself would handle death when it came. His mom and pop were the lights of his young life and I wondered if perhaps that day, on that golf course, he was learning a completely different lesson in life.

We learn from watching, listening, feeling, sensing, but will never know how we ourselves will handle death until it arrives on our own doorstep.

chapter twenty-one

don't you feel the spirit?

Has my father's death changed me? Absolutely. And for all time. It has made me look at everyone around me in a different light, made me listen to the wind and watch the colors of the sky, feel the softness of a baby's cheek, and recognize my own vulnerability. Since I now know, for a fact, that death does come knocking, I want to take advantage of every second I have with everyone I love. I want to hear their stories and absorb their pain and let them know how I feel about them. It's a knee-jerk reaction, for sure, but perhaps one long overdue.

One night, a year after my father's death, I called John, the cameraman with whom I worked for nearly fifteen years. He was there for all the Masters golf tournaments in Augusta we covered together, battling his way through the crowds to get the perfect picture, there for all the U.S. Opens and PGA Championships, the World Series, Super Bowls, half-a-hundred *Sporting Life* shoots. Working with me one week in the tragic squalor of Venezuela and, a week later, in a million-dollar home with Jack Nicklaus. We weren't specifically a team, for I worked with other cameramen off and on over the years, but we shared a thousand stories, argued and fussed, and made magical television. He was often my producer as well as my shooter, stepping from behind the camera for a moment to play devil's advocate, questioning a fact or suggesting another tack.

Now that I had changed positions, moving from one tower to another in our enormous complex, I no longer worked with him and saw him hardly at all. His father was dying, as they all eventually must, but his death was supposedly more imminent than most, and I called to check on how my friend's dad was doing. Before I lost my own father, I doubt that I would have done that one simple little exercise that took no more than a few minutes. I didn't want to face the emotions, didn't want to hear his pain. But I now wanted to know. And I wanted him to know that there were friends out there supporting him. I needed that during my own process. We all do.

We had shared a moment at the U.S. Open golf championship at Pinehurst, North Carolina, the summer before my father died, while his dad was still in moderately good health. I had done a story for our Father's Day show on how some of the golfers either react to being away on that holiday or enjoy having their fathers or offspring around them. I prepared to do a closing standup by the famous putting green there, and as I stood before the camera, microphone in hand, words at the ready, nothing would come. I tried one take and made it through half a sentence. I tried again . . . and nothing. I knew my dad was dying, knew what this day had meant to the two of us over the years, and I simply could hardly catch my breath. Tears filled my eyes.

I motioned to John to shut down the camera. Both he and my producer knew what I was going through, understood and said nothing, simply flipped a switch and waited. I turned my back and walked away, taking myself by the shoulders and shaking myself into attention.

Finally, after the long silence, I came back, nodded to John, and managed to get one right. It was stilted and uncomfortable and very difficult but I got one in the can and that would be plenty. We usually did backups, just in case, but one was more than enough this day.

John said later that he knew what I was going through and it was okay. He knows even better now. And with my call, I wanted to let him know that it was all right to back away, take a few deep breaths and try again.

We spent far too many Father's Days away from our own over the years, tried to make up for it with phone calls and gifts from faraway U.S. Opens. That thought attached itself deep inside me when my father died. And I'm certain it did inside John when his dad finally passed away fourteen months later. We do what we have to do. In fact, too many Mother's Days have been spent by both of us hundreds of miles away at another golf tournament in Augusta. That Mother's Day happened to almost always fall either on the final Sunday of the Masters or Father's Day on the final day of the U.S. Open is mere coincidence. The days are simply reminders, conveniently built by the world's greeting-card salesmen, when in fact every day should be Mother's and Father's Day. But try selling your mother or father that fact on the rare occasion of a forgotten call . . . or to your soul in the hours of mourning.

John and I share a quiet knowledge of the spirit world and that will help us both through all we experience. I think for a while, he simply humored me as I meandered through my musings every spring at Augusta National when we covered the Masters golf tournament together. It became an annual rite of passage to hear the whispers along Amen Corner, to sense the past. There is no place, at least in the golf world, that can rival Augusta National in April. The dogwoods and azaleas seem primed for the opening. And everywhere you turn, there is a piece of history waiting. It is a bit like Fenway

Park in Boston, Lambeau Field in Green Bay, Wembley Stadium in London. Close your eyes and sense the long flannels of yesteryear.

"Don't you feel the ghosts, John?" I would ask every April. "They're everywhere."

He would simply peek out from behind his camera and smile at me, as though I were a bit daft, and then return to his taping. In truth, Augusta National was built on land that was once, hundreds of years before, an Indian burial ground before it became a plantation and then a tree nursery. Certainly the rumblings of the past were swirling through the stately old Georgia pines, reminding us all to be gentle, be deferential. *Let us have our say.*

John thought little, if anything, about my mumblings until one Easter Sunday dawning. We were preparing to shoot our live weekly golf show behind the wonderful old Augusta clubhouse, under that ancient spreading oak. I was sitting on a stool, miked and ready, trying to memorize my opening lines. Could Greg Norman finally hold on to a third-round lead and win this event? He had a big enough lead this time; surely he wouldn't fold. As I was settling into a rhythm, two minutes to air, a strange and wool-thick mist suddenly began to blossom to my left, down off the eighteenth fairway, marching up the hill like an ominous curtain. It had been crystal clear and stunning just moments before but now, the darkness was returning.

I recognized the moment for what it was, threw out my old opening, and told the boys in the TV truck to be prepared because I was going to ad-lib my way into the show. I told them about the fog, which would soon overtake us all.

And then, under cue, on the air, I told the audience about this rising cloud, summoning the memories of wonderful men gone by. Why, I said, you could almost see the image of the great Bobby Jones hobbling by. But back to the present. Let's take a look at the third-round action from Saturday . . .

When we had finished the half hour, I was taking off my microphone when an older man opened a dormer window on the clubhouse to my right and shouted down to me.

"I gotta hand it to you, son," he said in that familiar Augusta twang. "How'd you get ol' Bobby to do that?"

And then he laughed and shut the window.

John stepped out from behind the camera and nodded.

"It was the strangest thing I've ever seen. I have no idea where he came from and I couldn't stop him from walking through the shot. You gotta go look at the tape in the truck."

And as I watched myself on videotape rambling about the ghost of Bobby Jones, an older man appeared behind me in the mist, hobbling slowly past on his cane, bent over and dressed in the garb of yesteryear. He was only there for a few seconds but he was as plain as the fog would allow. What the great Bobby Jones might have looked like, had he escaped the wheelchair and the death sentence years before. Happenstance? A spirit?

Do I believe my father is an angel now? And what exactly is an angel? Has he sprouted wings or is he simply a spirit, a guiding force, someone, some *thing* to watch over me? Did I say "simply"? What a poor choice of words, for such a dynamic gathering of electricity must be one of God's greatest gifts to us. Is Dad's presence still with us? Is that the essence of an angel? I vote yes. To all the above.

I have always felt that those with the purest of hearts return to us after death, to place unseen hands upon our shoulders and guide us. God's helpers, as it were. Guardian angels, some say. That may be terribly naive, and it probably is inconsistent with the Scriptures, but it's what I have thought for so many years. I like to think that my father's spirit is very evident around me and in how I live my life. I consider it his parting gift to me and I will forever be blessed because of it.

I have asked often of the sky, for that seems to be where my father is now (there, or the trees or the passenger seat), for answers to the mysteries of his dying days. Who was the white shadow next to his bed? If that voice telling him to return from his walk to heaven was really a woman's, as he thought, was she God? Did his grandfather notice the expressways as he looked down? Any surprises? Anybody he was expecting who isn't there, and vice versa? Has he remembered how to turn the copper wire into wind-blown trees again? Does he still need his glasses, his hearing aids, his teeth?

Are the streets truly gold and who coaches the football team, someone like Knute Rockne or Vince Lombardi? Does Casey Stengel manage the baseball team? Does Bronco Nagurski now block for Walter? And who's the reigning club champion—Ben Hogan? Bobby Jones? Or has Payne Stewart taken charge already?

Does he miss us as much as we miss him?

The lights just flickered.

The branches rustled.

Those are all the answers I will get . . . but perhaps all I will need.

epilogue

■ DECEMBER 2000

Dad? You out here tonight? I know, I know, seems like I always come out here on the deck to talk to you. But that's where we had so many great conversations while you were alive. You'd sit over there while I was barbecuing. Or we'd just stand, shoulder to shoulder, watching the ducks march up from the lake for their afternoon bread break. Now I'm always looking up to that one patch of sky between the two tallest pine trees to find you. Makes no sense, I know, but you know I'm a creature of habit and that's where I think you might be.

Dad, we need to talk. I don't know how much you get around these days. There's a good stretch of property to cover from here in Atlanta to where Mom lives in Maryland and no matter how fast you can travel these days, I don't know if you can be in two places at one time. I guess I'm stalling here a little so I'll get right to the point.

You know Mom is seeing another man?

You spoiled her, you know. You spent so much time with her when you were alive, every hour of every day and night, that when you died, she really missed the companionship. Oh, I don't mean she didn't miss *you*; she did and she still does. That will never change. But in the bigger picture, she misses having somebody around to talk to, to watch television with, to fuss over and take care of. The male-female ratio at that complex, you know, isn't real balanced. What, 90 percent women? All over sixty-five. And she was getting pretty tired of sitting around with the other older ladies, hearing their stories over and over and over again.

So one night a while back, she quietly told Chuck and Pam that she wanted some male companionship. Now, you know, don't get the wrong idea. She likes to be around men, just like you enjoyed being around women. There's a strange kind of bond there that my humble dabblings in psychology can't explain, but at the same time, I understand it. In fact, I'm guessing if the shoe had been on the other foot and she had died first, you yourself would be taking numbers and interviewing prime candidates about now. You'd have gone certified long ago, I'll bet, living alone. Couldn't cook, couldn't do laundry, couldn't figure out the bank statement, couldn't get along without having someone around to talk to, laugh with. You remember that now, hear, before you start getting all jealous.

I'm beating around the bush here, aren't I? Okay, okay.

So this guy moves in upstairs at the complex. Thus began one of the most perplexing, astonishing soap operas I've ever been on the edge of. Good-looking older man, eighty, used to work at the Smithsonian Institution in D.C., lost his wife a while back. Has family in the area too. Lotsa similarities to Mom's situation. Has all his hair still, is a runner, has a computer, seems pretty young for eighty.

Now, I wasn't there so I have no firsthand knowledge of this, Dad, but I guess the scramble for fresh meat was something to behold. All the older ladies sprucing up for the first time in years, batting their eyelashes and wondering if they could bring him dinner or help clean his place. But it seems he has eyes only for the younger redhead down in 108. And she? Well, he was the answer to a lotta prayers, it seems. Not that she had been praying for another man, don't get me wrong. It's just that the loneliness had become claustrophobic and the days so very long since you left. All she had to concern herself with was, well, herself. It's a bit like when you're lying in bed in the wee small hours, unable to sleep, and you feel a little twinge of pain. Because it's just you and your thoughts in the darkness, that twinge escalates into anything your fertile mind wants to imagine. In the light of morning, of course, it's just a pain that is long gone. But for a while there, it was cancer in your mind. That's a bit of the way Mom was getting, so alone with her thoughts and fears and concerns that they were growing way out of proportion.

But suddenly, she feels wonderful. Suddenly, there is someone else to worry over, someone else to stare out the window with and watch the snow fall. They appear to be a match, Dad, and I know you two had a few talks about this before you died. That you both joked about which one of you would wind up finding someone else if the other died. You allowed that it was okay with you if she did. Whether that was simply deathbed talk or you really meant it, I guess only you know.

It was strange for Chuck and me, I guess you know. Another man in Mom's life? Our immediate reaction, of course, was being flabbergasted. How could she possibly consider another man after nearly seven decades with Dad? It was the last thing we ever figured. We weren't as much upset as we were simply astonished. But as the days wore on, I found that many other men and women my age were going through the same startling transition with one parent or another. One particular afternoon, while I was playing golf with three new acquaintances, the subject arose as we walked the fairways.

"Oh, mine too," one player immediately piped up. "In fact, she's bringing her 'boyfriend' to our house for the holidays. We don't know whether to give them separate bedrooms or not. It's a funny problem."

"My dad just went into an assisted-living home," said another, "just a couple of weeks ago, and he's already had four dates. It's amazing. I never thought he'd ever get over losing my mother and here he is, dazzling all the girls with his style."

"Shoot, my dad died when he was fifty-seven," the third member of our foursome began, "and my mom's now ninety and has remarried twice since. Outlived 'em both and she's still looking."

"Take it as a good sign," came the encouragement.

And once we collected ourselves and gave it some thought, we did just that. Though for the most part, Dad, I must admit that I handled it pretty poorly.

"It means," Chuck told me on the phone one of the first nights after he found out, "that she's healthy."

She's healthy and she's vital and her ego, which had taken such a pounding these last few years, has received a gigantic boost. After all, this was the woman who competed in the Mrs. America contest. This is the woman who, for years, was thought to be my sister, not my mother. This is the woman who took such pride in her appearance and the way others saw her. And then her feet began to fail her and she had to adopt first the cane and then the walker, and then you got sick; things just began to collapse around her. But think about this, Dad: she wins the battle for this new guy! Even if she didn't participate in the war, she still won. Think how good that fact alone must be for her ego. She wouldn't ever admit that and will probably scold me royally for having told you. But it's true.

So she's healthy inside again and she has a man in her life. You'll love the card she sent us, Dad. I don't think she'd mind if I read some of it to you.

I'm so happy, I can't tell you! Phil [that's his name, Dad] *came last night for dinner when Nan was here. She likes him and says he reminds her of Poppa in his mannerisms—not looks. He is tall, thin, has a full head of white hair. He seems to care* very much *for me. He will be eighty-one in July. He is Scotch, graduated from Lafayette College and has been the keeper of the "Nation's Attic" at the Smithsonian.*

We went to the Mall today. He seems to want to go wherever I go and is concerned about my being away. [That sound familiar, Dad?] *We came home and folded my Christmas letters and stuffed them and he took them to the Post Office.*

We're going out for dinner and then he has a family thing tomorrow. He comes in the evening and we watch TV. Really great! I told Chuck I feel like a teenager!? Please forgive the dizzy old lady!!

Much Love, Mom

Three nights after we got her card, she called and it was the most invigorating conversation I think I've ever had with her.

"I'm in love," she gushed to me. "I just can't believe how God answered my prayers, but He did. I wasn't asking for anything but someone to share time with, talk to, eat dinner with, watch television, you know. But He gave me so much more.

"I feel like a young girl again."

I must admit, Dad, I was taken aback. I was happy for her but this was so, well, so *sudden*. I mean, she'd only known the guy a month. But I guess when you're that age you don't need to waste time in a prolonged engagement. I thought about asking if she and Phil would mind taking a test to see if they were suited for each other but thought that might be a bit too subtle reminder of the long ago so I let it slide. In truth, I was struggling for words, but fortunately, she had enough for the two of us.

"I think we're gonna get married; just a small ceremony at a chapel. Nothing big. Sometime in the spring. Do you believe that? You want a new father?"

Not particularly, but what I wanted made little difference. It was what *she* wanted that counted and this was something she obviously wanted a lot.

"He's got a full head of white hair, you know," she reminded me.

"Yeah, you wrote that in your card the other day."

"Oh, I did? I forgot. I'm so head over heels in love, it's just unbelievable. He worked for the Smithsonian for years."

"Uh-huh."

"And he's got a touch of dementia, I think, just like Dad had. He can be forgetful. But I guess we have that in common, too, huh?"

There was a huge, giddy sigh as she caught her breath.

"I worried a bit about how you would react to this. Are you okay with it?" she asked.

I told her that I couldn't be happier for her, that she certainly didn't need my approval but she had it, just the same.

"You're right." She laughed. "I'm no sixteen-year-old girl, although I wonder sometimes. I'm nearly seventy-seven and I can make up my own mind about things. But it's still important to me how you and Chuck feel."

"Just as long as you don't want me to give you away, Mom. I think I might have a tough time with that. But you're sure this is the right thing?"

"I've never been surer. You know, it's a different kind of love. Your dad and I just sorta drifted into love, over our youth. This was a bolt out of the blue. Not that one's better than the other, just very different.

"And I've been so very lonely. Your dad and I did everything together. They said we were Velcroed at the hip. And when he died,

I lost a part of me. There was a huge vacuum that wasn't filled until, well, Phil suddenly came into my life."

Life can be strange and twisted. That's one way of describing what has happened. Another might be, "The Lord works in mysterious ways." Either one works, for you see, Dad, this story has more twists and turns and stomach churns than any amusement park ride. Chuck and I both were worried about the suddenness of all this, and about the dementia that we learned later was Alzheimer's. We didn't want to dampen her enthusiasm, didn't want to rain on what would be her grandest parade, but we tried to subtly caution her. That's not easy when you're dealing with a seventy-six-year-old teenager, but then, you probably realized that a long time ago, right, Dad? She seemed to be setting herself up for another fall.

"Are you sure?" we asked again and again.

"Absolutely. And so what if we only get six months of happiness? That's better than six months of nothing, right? I can take care of him."

But that changed the very day the calendar tumbled into 2001. I won't go into the details, Dad; you probably know them already. But she found herself in an emergency room again, like the ones you two spent so much time in during the final months. And she saw what his disease could do, where it could go, how it could hurt. So painful, so lonely, so ugly. And just as quickly as this whole thing blossomed, it curled up around the edges and began to decay.

"We won't marry," she told me by phone the next morning, through the tears of heartbreak. "I can't go through that again. You and Chuck were right; you were trying to protect me and I just couldn't see it. I guess I'm not as young as I thought I was."

I felt so bad for her, Dad. She had been so very happy, so childlike, so much in love. We theorized that perhaps she was in love with being in love, but decided there wasn't much wrong with that if it produced the kind of radiant glow she had been wearing.

"You're wrong, Mom," I told her and then tried to tiptoe around the clichés. "You've just proved to yourself that there is plenty of spark left, that the fire hasn't died. Keep your eyes peeled and the casseroles ready. Another one might come along."

She laughed a little, not much.

"I still love him, you know? I just . . ."

And a few days later, they had reconciled . . . to the point of marriage again. He will move into an assisted-living home where they can keep a close eye on him. And since she can't move there with him, Mom will remain where y'all lived. But they'll be married. Go figure.

"That's so . . . so strange," I managed after hearing the latest installment.

"It's not strange," she replied, hurt that I would think so. "It happens every day. He got down on his knees and begged me to marry him, to take his name. And I am going to."

So it appears this new love they have discovered will continue, no matter what. I've felt like a counselor, Dad, and not a very good one. Every day is a new chapter. Who'd have thought it, right?

Well, it's getting cold out here, Dad. I'd better go in. I just thought you'd like to know how she's doing. I've tried to keep you up to date over the last year or so because I know how worried you were, leaving her behind, alone.

Why don't you pay her a visit, hold her hand, tell her it's all right? Funny, she said she hadn't talked to you much over the months since you've been gone, but she also said she asked you if it was okay, you know, her and Phil. And she said that you said fine. She needs you more than ever now, your presence, your spirit, your age-old love. I have a feeling the time they're going to have to spend apart is going to be excruciating for her. She needed someone, in the beginning, just to watch TV with, to read with, to eat dinner with, and now she marries a guy who has to live somewhere else. Must be love, huh?

I'll be back in touch again, soon as I have anything more to report. I hope it's better news next time. And the way things have been going, you'd better stay tuned because I'll probably be back with you quickly.

Funny thing, Dad; I keep looking for you between those two big pines by the lake but I could just as well shut my eyes and talk to you, for I know where you really live.

Strange how I fretted for so long about the right way to say goodbye to you when you really weren't going anywhere at all.

See you later, pal.

acknowledgments

How can I possibly find the words to thank those who have somehow hitched their wagons to this blistering star of mine these last months, who understood the glassy gaze in these eyes to be a kind of inspiration only divinely directed? Carol, who has been through everything with me over the decades, first and foremost, refilling the coffee cup and the creative passion on an hourly basis. Andrew Stuart, the literary agent who found a way to believe in this project from the very beginning. Brian Hampton, the editor who gave me balance and rein. The memories of *Sporting Life* subjects long relegated to a dusty video library, back to life one more time here. The book is titled *A Thousand Goodbyes,* but I can only pass along "A Million Thank-You's."

about the author

Jim Huber is the Emmy Award–winning essayist and commentator for Turner Sports—TNT and TBS—covering Wimbledon, NASCAR, the NBA, golf tournaments, and figure-skating competitions. He was with CNN for sixteen years, during which time he won a national Emmy and two CableAce Awards and an Edward R. Murrow Award. He's been in the media through newspapers, radio, and television since 1964. He and his wife, Carol, have been married for thirty-five years and have one son, Matthew.